BEING WATCHED

Being Watched

Legal Challenges to Government Surveillance

Jeffrey L. Vagle

NEW YORK UNIVERSITY PRESS

New York

For Kathy

NEW YORK UNIVERSITY PRESS
New York
www.nyupress.org
© 2017 by New York University
All rights reserved

References to Internet websites (URLs) were accurate at the time of writing. Neither the author nor New York University Press is responsible for URLs that may have expired or changed since the manuscript was prepared.

Library of Congress Cataloging-in-Publication Data
Names: Vagle, Jeffrey L., author.
Title: Being watched : legal challenges to government surveillance / Jeffrey L. Vagle.
Description: New York : New York University Press, [2017] | "Also available as an ebook." | Includes bibliographical references and index.
Identifiers: LCCN 2017010852| ISBN 9781479809271 (cl ; alk. paper) | ISBN 1479809276 (cl ; alk. paper)
Subjects: LCSH: Electronic surveillance—Law and legislation—United States. | Searches and seizures—United States. | Privacy, Right of—United States. | Locus standi—United States.
Classification: LCC KF5399 .V44 2017 | DDC 345.73/052—dc23
LC record available at https://lccn.loc.gov/2017010852

New York University Press books are printed on acid-free paper, and their binding materials are chosen for strength and durability. We strive to use environmentally responsible suppliers and materials to the greatest extent possible in publishing our books.

Manufactured in the United States of America

10 9 8 7 6 5 4 3 2 1

Also available as an ebook

CONTENTS

1

You Are Being Watched

It was not long after the events of September 11, 2001, and the subsequent actions of the United States and its allies, that Joanne Mariner began to suspect that her government was spying on her.[1] Her concern was not without foundation. As an attorney and deputy director of the Americas Division at Human Rights Watch (HRW), she had been doing research on the legal issues surrounding the U.S. government's covert policies adopted as part of its "global war on terrorism," including the CIA practice of "extraordinary renditions" and the decision to house some prisoners at a detention camp at the Guantanamo Bay Naval Base, located on the southeastern coast of Cuba. In 2004 Mariner was asked to chair a working group within HRW to come up with a strategic plan to address the growing list of human rights issues emerging from the global war on terrorism. As a result of the working group's research, HRW formed a new Terrorism and Counterterrorism Center in 2005. In 2006 Mariner was appointed the center's director.

Among the first findings of HRW's new Terrorism Center was the revelation that the CIA was operating secret prisons at "black sites" in countries such as Afghanistan, Poland, and Romania, where access and oversight of prison conditions could more easily be limited and controlled. As its research into these secret prisons expanded, HRW began to discover instances of CIA prisoner abuses, and this became a focal point for Mariner's work. From 2006 through 2009, she spent much of her time traveling around the world tracking down former CIA prisoners and trying to convince them to speak with her about the abuses they witnessed and suffered while they were held at these black sites. During this time, she spoke with many former detainees, who related some of the shocking stories of torture and abuse that were later confirmed in the 2014 U.S. Senate Select Committee on Intelligence (SSCI) report, *Committee Study of the Central Intelligence Agency's Detention and Interrogation Program*, commonly known as the Torture Report.[2]

Mariner and her team traveled extensively during this period, speaking not only with former detainees, but also with witnesses, experts, scholars, political activists, foreign government officials, and other HRW staff, discussing highly sensitive information, sometimes related to terrorism and counterterrorism, and often relating to U.S. foreign affairs. As this work progressed, it became increasingly obvious to Mariner and others at HRW that the CIA—and others within the U.S. government— would be highly interested in knowing the details of these communications, and she harbored few doubts that their communications would be monitored at every opportunity.

This was not a surprising conclusion for Mariner to reach. By the mid-2000s, stories began to surface telling of the mass interception of telecommunications by the U.S. intelligence community and, by extension, its partners in the "Five Eyes" signals intelligence–sharing alliance, comprising the United Kingdom, Canada, Australia, New Zealand, and the United States. Rumors about the breadth and depth of the ultra-secretive NSA's data collection activities had long existed, but without evidence of these programs, these rumors were largely dismissed as the paranoid fantasies of the tinfoil hat community. The 1998 film *Enemy of the State*, a high-tech thriller starring Will Smith, depicted the NSA as an omniscient, power-hungry government body that is willing to kill in order to enhance and protect its power, and has at its instantaneous command nearly limitless technological resources with which to track and control its enemies (one of which happens to be Will Smith's character). The premise of the film, while entertaining, was discounted by intelligence and technology experts as far-fetched, as it was generally agreed that the feats described in *Enemy of the State* would require technological capabilities far beyond anything the real-world NSA could muster. And besides, there were laws preventing foreign intelligence agencies like the NSA and CIA from spying on U.S. citizens, right? The rumors of a technologically powerful NSA with the ability to surveil the communications of every U.S. citizen seemed utterly implausible. To understand how these once fanciful or paranoid stories began to take hold among rational thinkers like Joanne Mariner, however, we turn to the story of Room 641A.

Just about the time Mariner and her colleagues were beginning their research on terrorism and counterterrorism for HRW, a technician named Mark Klein, then working for the global telecommunications giant AT&T, noted the construction of a new room in AT&T's Folsom Street networking facility in San Francisco.[3] This room, numbered 641A, was being built immediately adjacent to the room containing a 4ESS switch, a powerful computer switching system that was used to direct long-distance telephone calls through the Folsom Street facility. The facility also held the infrastructure that provided AT&T's WorldNet Internet service, international and domestic Voice Over IP (VoIP) telephony services, and data transport service to Asia and the Pacific Rim. The information flow moving through the Folsom Street facility was not a mere trickling headwaters—it was an Amazon of data.

Room 641A, known in AT&T documents as the SG3 Secure Room, was secretly built and equipped in 2002 for the NSA. NSA agents made repeated visits to the Folsom Street facility in 2002 and 2003 to supervise the work. Unlike access to other rooms in the facility, access to Room 641A was limited to a handful of AT&T employees who had been personally cleared by the NSA. The AT&T technicians who were expected to service and maintain the equipment in the facility had master keys to every room but Room 641A. The extremely limited access to 641A began to cause problems at the facility. In 2003 a large industrial air conditioner in the secure room began to leak water, which eventually began leaking onto the equipment housed on the floor beneath it. Sensitive electronic equipment does not react well to water, and there was a risk of interrupting customer services and causing untold damage to AT&T's expensive communications facility. But because access to 641A was limited to only a few AT&T employees—who did not necessarily work at or near the Folsom Street facility—it took days before a cleared technician arrived to enter the secure room and repair the faulty air conditioner. With the attendant inconvenience, risk, and expense of such a secretive endeavor, why was the NSA so interested in the AT&T Folsom Street facility? The answer can easily be seen in the facility's function as a choke point through which vast amounts of communications information was forced to flow at scales unimaginable until it was discovered that light could be harnessed to transmit information over ultrathin strands of glass.

Copper wire had long been the favorite medium of telecommunications companies for transmitting electric signals. Due to its high electrical conductivity, strength, and ease of handling, copper was (and is) an excellent material for this purpose. One of the limitations of copper wire for telecommunications, especially transoceanic communication, was its inability to cleanly propagate electrical signals across long distances without the use of multiple repeaters—essentially, signal boosters—along the way. Relatedly, copper was also prone to "leak" electromagnetic energy, and was vulnerable to interference from other sources of electromagnetic radiation unless the copper was properly shielded from this interference. In the 1970s, advances in the manufacture of optical fiber—clear, flexible strands of extruded glass or plastic that used light to transmit information—made this medium an attractive alternative to copper. Optical fiber was electrically nonconductive, and was therefore not vulnerable to electromagnetic interference issues. Signal loss over long distances was orders of magnitude lower with optical fiber versus copper. Telecommunications companies such as AT&T quickly began replacing their long-haul copper wiring with optical fiber.

The switch from copper to optical fiber expanded not only the reach of land-based telecommunications, but also its capacity. The vast amount of data transmitted globally in our current information economy would not be possible without the enormous amounts of bandwidth available using optical fiber technology. Optical fiber can handle huge amounts of data. A single optical fiber alone can transmit three million full-duplex telephone calls or over ninety thousand television channels. The fiber bundles used at the Folsom Street facility typically consisted of ninety-six of these fibers, and multiple sets of these fiber bundles created a high-speed "common backbone" for data transmission, making the Folsom Street facility a major information hub that linked other such facilities across the world. The facility therefore handled all AT&T data going to and from the Pacific Rim, and there was a lot of it. If someone could tap into this vast river of information at this point, it would provide an extremely efficient means of eavesdropping on a significant portion of U.S. domestic and international communications. But while the Folsom Street facility offered an attractive opportunity, a potential eavesdropper was first faced with two technical—and one legal—hurdles. First, it was not a straightforward process to "tap" optical fiber, as it had been for copper wire. Second, doing any sort of useful analysis on the vast amounts of data flowing through the facility would require unheard-of amounts of computing horsepower and algorithmic complexity. Finally, the third-party tapping of private telephone conversations or electronic communications is generally illegal for private entities, and even government access is tightly controlled to protect citizens' privacy. Even government agencies had to jump through certain legal hoops to intercept domestic communications. The NSA, however, had developed its own answers to all of these questions.

First, how does one go about tapping fiber optic cable? In the old days, when copper cables were the only method of transmitting wire line communication, the job was relatively simple. Since copper used electrical signals to transmit information, it conducted small amounts of electrical energy along its length, some of which "leaked" or radiated outward from the cable as electromagnetic energy. If eavesdroppers wanted to listen in on the information passing over a copper wire, they only needed to wrap some sort of passive device around the cable that could absorb this leaked energy, thus gaining access to the information passing over the copper cable without actually disturbing the original electrical circuit. Tapping fiber optic cable is not nearly this straightforward, since optical fiber does not use electricity to transmit information, but instead uses light.[4] One would need to wrap the transparent core of the optical fiber with a cladding material that has a lower refractive index than the core material. This construction causes the light to propagate through the fiber by reflecting off the cladding material, and is therefore kept completely within the optical fiber's core. This means that any information passed through the fiber via light pulses is visible only at the two ends of the unbroken fiber—no information is "leaked" through the optical fiber's cladding. This means that any would-be fiber optic eavesdropper must be able to physically cut and splice the fiber in order to listen in on the transmitted information.

Splicing optical fiber requires a level of expertise far beyond merely cutting two cables and twisting their ends together, as one might do with copper wiring. It is an expensive process that requires specialized equipment and can be quite intrusive in a busy hub like the Folsom Street facility, where vast amounts of customer data were already flowing through its optical fiber bundles. Further, the NSA did not wish simply to intercept the information being transmitted over these fibers, but to "split" the signals into two identical copies, one of which would go to its original destination, and the other would be routed to NSA equipment. Just as dividing the flow of water through plumbing reduces the downstream capacity of the original pipes, this "splitting" of light pulses through AT&T's optical fibers also reduced their downstream signal strength. Such an operation required careful planning, and a small group of cleared AT&T technicians—one of whom was Mark Klein—was brought in to assist the NSA in this complex task. As an expert in these matters, Klein was asked to review the NSA's "Cut-In and Test Procedure" documents that articulated its plan to split the Folsom Street facility's fiber optic signals, with one branch of the resulting split going directly to Room 641A. While reviewing these documents, Klein noticed that the plan allowed the NSA to capture the optical signals from the facility's peering links, which meant that the NSA would receive communications information not only from AT&T customers but also from all non-AT&T customers who used these links. Through his review of the NSA's cut-in and splicing plans for the Folsom Street facility, Klein recognized that the NSA was giving itself a direct tap into AT&T's communications backbone.

The second technical hurdle to eavesdropping on an information hub like the Folsom Street facility was the challenge of making sense of the enormous flow of data in real time. That is, if the NSA wanted to conduct even the most superficial of analyses in this fast-flowing river of communications information, it would need computational capacities and analytical algorithms generally unknown to the commercial world at the time. But this problem fell right into the NSA's sweet spot. It had long been known to deploy "acres" of the fastest and most powerful computers in the world, and as Moore's Law continued to hold true, the NSA wielded untold-of depths of computing power within smaller and smaller footprints. Further, the NSA was known to be one of the biggest employers of mathematics, physics, and computer science PhDs in the world. This much concentrated brainpower was likely to yield computational techniques and algorithms that would put commercially available software and firmware to shame. The exact details behind the NSA's analytical capabilities are highly classified, of course. Mark Klein was given a glimpse into the NSA's design for the Folsom Street facility, however, through his review of its "cut-in" plans. Some of the equipment being loaded into Room 641A included high-end Sun Microsystems servers, fast Juniper "backbone" traffic routers, a Narus STA 6400 "Semantic Traffic Analyzer," and a Narus Logic Server. In other words, Room 641A was being packed with some of the fastest, most powerful, and most sophisticated telecommunications processing and analytical gear then available. As we now know, the NSA's technology has given it the power to effect just the sort of deep-and-wide dragnet surveillance once dismissed as science fiction when depicted by Hollywood.

Before the NSA could move forward with its plan to tap all communications going through the AT&T Folsom Street facility, however, it had one final obstacle to overcome—the law. Since its creation by a secret presidential memorandum in 1952, the NSA's mission was to (a) strengthen U.S. signals intelligence capabilities, (b) support the nation's ability to wage war, and (c) generate information central to the conduct of foreign affairs. The NSA was meant to be an outward-facing agency, obtaining foreign intelligence through the intercept of foreign communications. Following the revelation of multiple serious illegal activities and other abuses by the U.S. intelligence community (IC) in the late 1960s and early 1970s (which will be explored in greater depth in later chapters), Congress enacted a new law—the Foreign Intelligence Surveillance Act (FISA)—to prevent future IC abuses by forbidding intelligence agencies from using foreign intelligence gathering as an excuse to conduct domestic surveillance. This law also placed four crucial limits on the nature of foreign intelligence gathering by the IC. First, the new law required all targets of foreign intelligence surveillance to be either a foreign power or an agent of a foreign power. Second, the law required that intelligence agencies show probable cause—a standard drawn from criminal law—that would demonstrate, with particularity, that the target to be placed under surveillance was a foreign power or an agent of a foreign power. Third, the law limited the basis of this probable cause to exclude activity otherwise protected by the First Amendment. Finally, the new law demanded that intelligence agencies draft and adhere to "minimization procedures" that would find and destroy all inadvertently collected data not related to foreign intelligence. After FISA was enacted, the intelligence agencies reluctantly accepted the restrictions as the new cost of doing business.

The terrorist attacks of September 11, 2001, however, made some members of executive branch question the FISA restrictions, reasoning that, in times of national crisis, the intelligence community had to "take the gloves off" in order to effectively do its job helping to protect the nation. FISA restrictions would slow down the intelligence-gathering process and would hamper efforts to identify and locate potential threats. Further, this new kind of asymmetrical warfare meant that the concepts of discrete battlefields and easily identifiable enemies were now antiquated. It was no longer practical to assume that threats would come from outside our nation's borders, and the intelligence community therefore needed to expand its brief to include all communication activity, foreign and domestic. In other words, the Bush administration reasoned that military and intelligence agencies now needed a free hand to conduct their business, and the peacetime rules no longer applied.

This reasoning was not done in public, however. For the intelligence agencies to conduct their business on the "dark side" (made necessary by this new kind of warfare), the administration also needed to operate in this fashion, and thus elected to treat all such discussions as privileged under the president's constitutional wartime powers. This philosophy meant that the unnecessary involvement of Congress or the courts would only serve to further damage U.S. defense posture—and the Bush administration at this critical point considered nearly all communication with Congress unnecessary. The challenge for the administration, therefore, was how to allow the NSA unfettered access to foreign and domestic communication without either applying for a court order (as required by FISA) or going to Congress for special authorization. Both options were likely to take more time than the Bush administration wanted to spend, and, given the extremely broad scope of information being sought, both stood a better than fair chance of denial. The only viable option the Bush administration recognized at this point was to plow ahead unilaterally under what it saw as its wartime powers.

Following this reasoning, President George W. Bush secretly authorized a number of covert intelligence collection activities following the September 11 attacks, collectively known as the President's Surveillance Program (PSP). All information gathered under PSP authorization was specially classified and compartmented to prevent outside knowledge of these activities. The administration knew that the courts and Congress would likely view the PSP as illegal without additional congressional authority, so secrecy was the order of the day. The secrecy of programs like the PSP is difficult enough to maintain when the only actors are themselves agents of the government. The problem is exacerbated when outsiders—like AT&T—are brought in to the equation. U.S. corporations have a long history of providing covert assistance to the government in times of crisis. Some of those activities have been legal, but many have occupied a legal gray area that the companies have been less than eager to make public or include in their corporate histories.

The U.S. legal system distinguishes between the government (along with its agents) and everyone else. Specifically, the constitutional rights and privileges found in the Bill of Rights apply only to government actors. Generally speaking, it is therefore not possible to hold corporations liable for violating the prohibition against unreasonable searches and seizures found in the Fourth Amendment. More plainly, unlike the government, Google can (and does) read your email sent through Google Mail without first having to obtain a judicial warrant, although it may be (and is) required under other statutes to disclose this fact somewhere in its terms and conditions. There are many reasons for this disparity, chief among which is the fact that we grant the government the power to arrest, imprison, and, in some cases, kill its citizens—powers we do not grant corporations. The drafters of the U.S. Constitution codified their suspicion of government power in order to curb the sorts of abuses world governments had engaged in fairly consistently up to that point. Thus, domestic law enforcement officers are required to seek permission from a court before searching or seizing our persons, homes, papers, or effects. In 1972 the U.S. Supreme Court held that this principle applied universally to any domestic surveillance targeting a domestic threat. This decision, coupled with FISA, meant that the NSA could not conduct domestic surveillance without first showing a court how that particular surveillance was directly tied to a foreign power or agent of a foreign power.

Thus, in 2005, when Mark Klein decided to leak to the press that he had discovered NSA secret dragnet surveillance activities in AT&T's Room 641A, civil rights organizations like the Electronic Frontier Foundation and the American Civil Liberties Union immediately took exception, filing actions on behalf of multiple plaintiffs against AT&T in 2006 and the NSA in 2008 in federal court. In the *Hepting v. AT&T* case, plaintiffs, all AT&T customers, claimed that AT&T had been acting as an agent of the government, and was therefore bound by the restrictions found in the First and Fourth Amendments.[5] In *Jewel v. NSA*, a different set of AT&T customers brought direct First and Fourth Amendment claims against the government agency.[6]

The facts surrounding the *Hepting* and *Jewel* cases drew worldwide attention. In fact, as reporting on the government's dragnet surveillance program expanded, documents emerged that told of secret NSA rooms in other telecommunications hub facilities, including Atlanta, San Jose, Los Angeles, San Diego, and Seattle. Other technical experts reviewed these documents and agreed that the plans showed an agreement between AT&T and the government to grant the NSA unfettered access to its telecommunications traffic. As one engineer put it, after noting the resources and expertise put into the NSA dragnet operation, "this is the correct way to do high volume Internet snooping."

When confronted about the program, Bush administration officials admitted that the NSA had indeed gained access to most of the telephone calls in the United States, but insisted that such a dragnet was necessary to catch the "bad guys." Specifically, in order to ensure that a potential target's full network of communication activity could be traced, "you'd have to have all the calls or most of them. But you wouldn't be interested in the vast majority of them." The government was thus arguing that, while the NSA may be collecting all or most of the telecommunications data in the United States, it promised only to look at the subset of that information that was relevant to its hunt for the "bad guys."[7] By 2007, however, the Bush administration began to recognize that the repeated reauthorization of the PSP on the basis of presidential wartime powers was wearing a bit thin, and sought to formalize its new model of surveillance through legislation.

In August 2007 Congress passed the Protect America Act, which expanded government surveillance authority by codifying many of the terms contained in the Bush administration's PSP activities from 2001 to 2007. Congress held no hearings on the proposed legislation, and the act was passed after only four days of debate. The new law contained a "sunset provision," however, which limited its life to six months. Recognizing the limited lifetime of this new surveillance authority, the Bush administration pushed for more permanent legislation, this time aiming to change the very law that laid out many of these restrictions in the first place—FISA. Like the Protect America Act and the PSP authorizations before it, the proposed permanent amendments to FISA would expand executive branch authority to conduct mass surveillance dragnets on U.S. citizens' international communications. While the proposed amendments kept in place certain restrictions on the direct domestic surveillance of U.S. citizens with no reasonable connection to foreign targets, the amendments would allow for the mass acquisition of communications even if all the data to be acquired originated or terminated within the United States. These changes became law under the FISA Amendments Act, signed by President Bush in July 2008.

As the news spread of the NSA's growing power to conduct dragnet surveillance operations, Joanne Mariner and her colleagues at Human Rights Watch began to worry. If the U.S. government can simply attach its listening devices to the country's telecommunications networks at will, without the approval of any court, without the approval of Congress, and without the knowledge of the American people, what was to stop it from expanding its search for "bad guys" to successively broader searches based only on the whim of a government agency (or agent)? Who within the government got to decide who was a "bad guy"? The government had a rather spotty record when it came to "bad guy" targeting, especially in times of crisis (real or imagined), and it had been agreed—again and again—that the labeling as "enemy" of a person or group of people was a process best done in the open. In 2008 Mariner and her colleagues were convinced that, given what had been revealed about the PSP, and the subsequent surveillance expansion under the FISA Amendments Act, they and their contacts were almost certainly targets of the intelligence community, and their communications were being intercepted and collected by the government.

In 2008 Mariner began discussing her concerns with attorneys she knew at the ACLU. In these discussions, she was not surprised to learn that other organizations in similar positions as Human Rights Watch were expressing the same fears. Attorneys, human rights workers, labor advocates, legal researchers, and media organizations were all beginning to read the writing on the wall regarding the government's new authority to conduct dragnet surveillance programs. All of these organizations regularly engaged in sensitive or privileged communications with clients, sources, witnesses, experts, foreign officials, and human rights victims across the globe, many of whom were likely to be monitored under the modified version of FISA. Those concerned were not naïfs. They understood very well—perhaps better than most—the dangers posed in this world, and supported the government's interest in keeping an eye on individuals who were reasonably thought to threaten the United States or its citizens. But they also understood that the Constitution had very clear things to say when it came to the surveillance of U.S. citizens and residents, and they therefore questioned the legal foundations upon which the FISA Amendments Act was based.

The ACLU agreed with Joanne Mariner's and others' assessments of the situation, and filed suit on behalf of multiple plaintiffs in the Southern District of New York, challenging the constitutionality of the FISA Amendments Act. The case, *Amnesty International et al. v. Clapper*, specifically took issue with the FISA Amendments Act's sweeping surveillance authorization, which no longer required a showing of probable cause that the intended target was a foreign power or agent of a foreign power.[8] In the eyes of the plaintiffs, the FISA amendments stripped away some of the most important safeguards specifically included in FISA by the original drafters to prevent the sort of abuses by the government that had once again emerged post-9/11. The *Amnesty* plaintiffs alleged in their complaint that, because of these broad—and unconstitutional— changes to FISA, they were forced to incur new expenses and jump through additional hoops in order to protect their private or privileged communications, and were thus harmed by this new legislation. Based on their allegations that the FISA amendments were unconstitutional, the *Amnesty* plaintiffs asked the court to grant them summary judgment. In U.S. courts, summary judgment allows a party before the court to ask the judge to rule on the law of the case, without the need for trial, if there are no disputes of material fact for the court to resolve. Here, the only material facts the *Amnesty* plaintiffs were alleging were the FISA amendments signed into law in 2008.

The government's response to the *Amnesty* plaintiffs' claims did not begin with a refutation of their claims. Rather, the government asserted that, as a threshold matter, the plaintiffs had no right to argue their case before the court. The government argued that, in effect, whether or not the plaintiffs' claims were valid did not matter—the court could not hear their arguments on the merits of the case, since the plaintiffs did not have *standing*. The district court judge agreed with the government. In a sixty-four-page decision, Judge John G. Koeltl ignored the plaintiffs' arguments on the merits, holding that the plaintiffs "lack[ed] Article III standing to bring [their] constitutional challenge to the [FISA Amendments Act]." Koeltl denied the *Amnesty* plaintiffs' motion for summary judgment and granted the government's motion, dismissing the complaint and closing the case.

The *Amnesty* plaintiffs appealed the district court's decision to the Second Circuit Court of Appeals, arguing that the lower court had erred when it held that the plaintiffs lacked standing to appear before the court. The Second Circuit Court agreed with the plaintiffs and reopened the case, sending it back to the district court to decide the summary judgment motions on their merits. In turn, the government petitioned the Second Circuit for a rehearing of the appeal *en banc*—a proceeding that requires every Second Circuit Court of Appeals judge to hear the appeal, rather than the three-judge panel that heard the original arguments. The Second Circuit denied this petition in September 2011, and the government turned to the Supreme Court.

The U.S. Supreme Court agreed to hear the case of *Clapper v. Amnesty International* (the order of the parties' names now reversed, since the government was now the moving party). The question before the Court did not concern the unconstitutionality of the FISA amendments, nor any other question regarding the merits of the *Amnesty* plaintiffs' case. The only question before the Court was whether the plaintiffs could demonstrate this seemingly magical property of Article III standing to even argue the merits of their summary judgment motion. The district court had held that the plaintiffs did not have it. The Second Circuit Court of Appeals said the plaintiffs *did* have it. In February 2013, Justice Samuel Alito delivered the majority opinion of the Court, holding that the district court had been correct—the plaintiffs had no standing to bring their case before any federal court.

At this point, many would likely be quite reasonably puzzled by this concept of standing. How is it possible that plaintiffs can have the courthouse doors shut in their faces before they have even had the chance to present their arguments to the judge? On its face, standing doctrine appears to be anathema to the American system of justice, where every citizen is entitled to his or her day in court. Where did this doctrine of standing come from? Can it be found in some statute? How could prospective plaintiffs know whether they had standing to begin with? Is it possible that a plaintiff with a valid legal complaint could be barred from asking any court for assistance? Of more specific concern to the *Amnesty* plaintiffs, could it be possible that challenges to unconstitutional government surveillance programs might fail before they even had a chance to succeed on their merits?

To answer these questions, we must first understand the legal basis upon which standing doctrine rests. I will address the details of this doctrine at greater length elsewhere in this book, but for our immediate purposes, we begin with the concept that all litigation begins with some kind of harm. The framers of the Constitution made plain this requirement in their provision for federal courts in Article III, which limits their jurisdiction to "cases" and "controversies," terms that we will explore more fully later in this book. This clause has always been interpreted to restrict federal courts to issues of actual harm, where there are identifiable adversaries—at least one of which has suffered actual injury due to actions or inactions of the other(s). Take away any one of these elements, and federal courts have no jurisdiction to hear the case as a threshold matter. Thus, if a plaintiff cannot demonstrate actual harm to the court, the judge cannot hear the case, since the plaintiff does not have standing. Standing doctrine is, of course, much more complex than this facile summary, and I will examine relevant portions of its rich history throughout this book.

The doctrine of Article III standing was no secret to the *Amnesty* plaintiffs and their attorneys, of course, while the exact parameters of that doctrine remain difficult to articulate, even for constitutional and federal court scholars. Standing doctrine has been referred to as the "Rorschach test of federal courts" for the tendency of individual judges to perceive the doctrine in uniquely different ways. Article III standing is so complex, in fact, that entire books can be—and have been—written on the topic. I will not attempt to replicate these efforts here, but will make reference to them throughout this work. My topic is narrower: How does standing doctrine affect challenges to government surveillance programs, and upon what foundation does this specific doctrine lie?

Case precedent for standing in surveillance cases has an interesting and flawed history. This jurisprudential family tree has many branches, of course, but one particular case stands out as a philosophical origin point. This case—the 1972 Supreme Court decision in *Laird v. Tatum*— provides both a precedential basis and an ideological and historical lens through which we can analyze the Court's current thinking on standing to challenge the legality of government surveillance programs. *Laird*, cited as a basis for both the district court's and Supreme Court's denial of standing to the *Amnesty* plaintiffs, was one of the principal watershed cases that led to the formation in 1974 of high-profile congressional public hearings on the problem of military domestic surveillance of U.S. citizens. The facts behind *Laird* are remarkably similar to those faced in *Amnesty* nearly four decades later. All the necessary pieces are present in this story: a country in crisis, overzealous military and intelligence agencies, a perception that enemies and subversives walk among us and need to be identified and rooted out in order to preserve the nation, a citizenry suspicious of government programs and motives, an ideologically fractured Supreme Court, technological advances that expanded surveillance opportunities, a whistle-blowing government employee, and a secretive presidential administration with a demonstrated willingness to ignore or circumvent the law when it felt it was necessary.

At its core, this book is meant as an examination of our constitutional democratic system of government and its ability to remain healthy and intact during times of national crisis. Governance has always been a series of trade-offs between freedom and organization. In order to provide for the welfare of its citizens, a government must be able to conduct surveillance at some level. For example, in order to prevent and control outbreaks of infectious disease, government agencies require information from hospitals, doctors, and other health care workers regarding the health of their patients. To prosecute suspected criminals, law enforcement agencies must have a mechanism through which they can legally collect the necessary information so as to make a case for the suspect's guilt. And health and welfare agencies require detailed demographic information in order to ensure that the government's finite resources are being put to the most effective use. All of this is to say that the word "surveillance" is, in itself, a neutral term. It has taken on negative connotations due to its more egregious uses (and abuses) by governments and other organizations through the ages, which tip the freedom-organization balance away from personal liberty toward increased—and sometimes total—government control.

The list of factors that go into the freedom-organization balance equation is long, and I have neither the space nor the inclination to address all of them in this book. Our aim, rather, is to understand how the amorphous judicial doctrine of Article III standing has become a seemingly insurmountable barrier to those wishing to challenge the constitutionality of government surveillance programs in federal courts. It will entail a journey through the constitutional basis for federal courts, a foray into the topic of judicial recusal, a history of military domestic surveillance in America, the natural tensions between the three branches of government, the powers of the presidency in times of war (and the role of Congress and the courts in regulating those powers), and the power of individual citizens in the ongoing quest for the elusive freedom-organization balance. We will take our first steps on this journey via a small (and now defunct) Army post in the southeastern corner of Baltimore known as Fort Holabird.

2

A History of Government Surveillance

The story of government surveillance in the United States is inextricably intertwined with the nation's history of military intelligence. The American ethos is one of profound ambivalence toward a standing army. Americans have had a love-hate relationship with military and police functions since the founding of the nation, and took steps to put limits on the powers of government to impose its will on its citizens through the illegitimate use of force. The very idea of a federal police force was anathema in the United States for well over its first century, until a campaign of fear over foreign anarchist uprisings combined with a bit of political subterfuge by Theodore Roosevelt's administration created the predecessor of what would become the Federal Bureau of Investigation.

The concern Americans shared over a too-powerful standing military or a centralized government police force came from the Founders' early experiences with British authority and later observations of police abuses in despotic states throughout the nineteenth century. Many of these abuses manifested themselves through surveillance activities, where secretive branches of a police force would engage in military-style intelligence activities against its own citizens. For example, the Russian Empire's Department for Protecting the Public Security and Order, commonly abbreviated as Okhrana, was originally formed to root out political terrorism and revolutionary activity, but quickly expanded its role to secretly monitor and suppress any person or group that the government deemed subversive. This use of internal intelligence operations for political ends against citizens was just what most Americans wished to avoid. These surveillance and intelligence activities were therefore best left to external military operations.

While the U.S. Army has long maintained personnel and units that served an intelligence function—that is, the gathering, analyzing, and dissemination of information necessary in the planning and execution of military missions—it was not until World War I that the Army established a school to formally train officers and enlisted personnel in the art of military intelligence. Until that time, Army leadership had been fairly indifferent toward the formation of a separate military intelligence corps and suspicious of formal military education, preferring instead to conduct all necessary intelligence functions "organically," within each military unit. In the late nineteenth century, an Army infantry colonel named Arthur L. Wagner took steps to change the Army's mind regarding the importance of military intelligence.

Colonel Wagner seemed a rather unlikely candidate for the job. Graduating from West Point in 1875 near the bottom of his class, and remembered mainly for his preference for reading military history rather than completing his course work, Wagner spent the early part of his career on the western American frontier, putting up telegraph lines, performing escort duty, and seeing some combat in the U.S. campaign against the Sioux and Nez Perce nations. Wagner's career progressed much like those of many other infantry officers at the time, but he began to distinguish himself from the herd in 1884, when he published an essay titled "The Military Necessities of the United States, and the Best Method of Meeting Them." The essay won a gold medal from the Military Service Institution of the United States, and garnered attention from Army brass. In 1886, when Wagner's regiment was reassigned to Fort Leavenworth, Kansas, his developing reputation as a military scholar preceded him, and he was appointed to the position of assistant instructor in the newly established Department of Military Art at the Army's Infantry and Cavalry School.

First Lieutenant Wagner flourished as a military instructor, joining with a few other progressively minded officers at Fort Leavenworth to transform the institution into the core of the Army's educational system, which today still supports the U.S. Training and Doctrine Command (TRADOC) through its Combined Arms Center. While teaching at Fort Leavenworth, Wagner recognized the need to establish a military science curriculum around a core set of texts, based on American experience in war, a somewhat radical idea within the decidedly Eurocentric Army at the time. Specifically, Wagner wished to incorporate the Army's hard-won experience gained during the American Civil War into the American military canon, a concept that met some resistance with the "Prusso-maniacs" within Army leadership.[1]

Wagner revived a moribund military education curriculum by introducing his style of applied military history, using historical examples as case studies to prompt students to think on their feet, avoiding rote answers and the canned responses of strict doctrine. He abhorred the Army's existing focus on military drill and administrative tasks, and worked to professionalize the Army officer corps through a rigorous study of military theory. Flexibility and problem-solving abilities were critical attributes to be honed by Wagner's students, and Wagner's texts were soon considered mandatory reading for all Army officers. George C. Marshall, the future chief of staff of the U.S. Army during World War II, and a former student of Wagner's, remarked that Wagner was "the first of our military men to write anything readable on tactics."[2]

In 1893 Wagner published a book titled *The Service of Security and Information*, where he made the argument for the establishment of a professional Army intelligence corps, stressing the importance of relevant, accurate battlefield information to the Army officer. The Army had, in fact, created its first military intelligence division in 1885, but it was only as a subordinate unit to the adjutant general, not as a command of its own. Wagner's book used multiple examples from Army history to illustrate the need for a professionally educated military intelligence corps, citing case after case where the existing intelligence model failed the Army, sometimes with catastrophic results. Wagner's thesis was that military security and military intelligence were inseparable concepts, and emphasized the need not just for intelligence, but also for *counter*intelligence.

Counterintelligence, with its use of spies, turncoats, informers, deserters, and general subterfuge, was thought of as ungentlemanly by most military schools of thought at the time, and its unseemliness made it the redheaded stepchild of military doctrine. But Wagner recognized the opportunities available to the military commander who was able to make use of such methods, and argued that it was impossible for a military commander to pay too much attention to these sources. Further, commanders must make every effort to protect their own secrets, lest opposing forces use these same methods on them. His book went into great detail on interrogating prisoners, gathering information from newspapers, using women as spies ("often the best of spies; but their means of gaining information is generally in direct proportion to their lack of character, and accordingly proportionate to their lack of credibility"), and tapping telegraph wires. Wagner's book was an early manual on what modern militaries refer to as the "intelligence preparation of the battlefield."

Wagner died in 1905, unsuccessful in his attempts to convince Army leadership of the need for a military intelligence corps. His teaching and scholarship had an enormous impact on his students, however, and a new generation of Army officers, educated by Wagner's revolutionary curriculum, began to institute changes in Army doctrine. In 1917, after years of persistent lobbying of the Army by Wagner's former students, a Military Intelligence (MI) Division was finally created, just in time to assist the Army as it entered the war in Europe. In 1918 Colonel Ralph Van Deman took over the MI Division, and instituted the first organized training regimen for intelligence officers, with the establishment of the U.S. Army Intelligence School within the AEF General Staff College at Langres, France. At the same time, the Army created what would eventually become the Counter Intelligence Corps, the Corps of Intelligence Police. Upon returning from France after the war, Colonel F. L. Dengler created the first U.S.-based intelligence training unit, widening the focus of the school beyond the parochial needs of the war in Europe. Following Wagner's model, great efforts were made to ensure that the hard-won lessons of World War I were not lost, but passed on to future intelligence officers and soldiers. The old stovepiping model of the Army's Military Intelligence Corps, where officers were organized and separated by discipline, was also broken down, opening the door for cross-training and general education of personnel.

During the interwar years, funds for intelligence training began to dry up, due in large part to the effects of the Great Depression on the nation's economic priorities. While the MI Division continued to publish textbooks and field manuals based on changing doctrine, the number of intelligence officers the division was able to train dropped precipitously, with only two officers trained each year from 1935 through the beginning of World War II. With the Japanese attack on the U.S. naval base at Pearl Harbor late in 1941, the Army quickly realized that it needed once again to shore up its intelligence capabilities. To meet this demand, the Army authorized the Military Intelligence Training Center (MITC), which began operations at Camp Ritchie, Maryland, in June 1942.

The Corps of Intelligence Police, redesignated the Counter Intelligence Corps (CIC), took over the Tower Town Club, a building near Chicago's Loop, and began training operations there in 1942. The CIC students went about their training in civilian attire, learning, among other things, to pick locks, lift fingerprints, forge documents, and tail suspects, not to mention judo and other hand-to-hand combat tactics. Once the CIC students had completed the course in Chicago, they were paired with a trained CIC special agent and given four weeks of practical training in the field. In June 1943 this staging took place at two Maryland bases: Camp Ritchie and Fort Holabird, a small Army post located within the city limits of Baltimore, originally built in 1917 to serve as a supply depot.

In 1944 the Army reorganized its military intelligence units, bringing the CIC branch under the MI Division under the control of the Army General Staff. The training of military intelligence officers and counterintelligence officers continued apace through the Korean War, but without a single training institution the MI Division could call its own. That ended in 1955, when the Combat Intelligence School at Fort Riley, Kansas, merged with the Counterintelligence School at Fort Holabird. This small post, wedged between factories in gritty, industrial Baltimore, became the home of Army military intelligence.

Americans' ambivalent attitude toward military surveillance and intervention in domestic civil affairs has produced a rather uneven history of internal military activity. Despite this national reticence, America's history is littered with examples of domestic military actions, some quite illegal or made illegal after the fact. For instance, the pre–Civil War South regularly used military troops—mostly state militia—to protect the institution of slavery by suppressing revolts, conducting slave patrols, and keeping an active watch out for budding insurrections and other slave conspiracies. Federal troops were sometimes called in, as well, perhaps most famously in the suppression of abolitionist John Brown's unsuccessful attempt to take over the federal arsenal at Harpers Ferry, Virginia, in 1859. The U.S. government's efforts to remove or exterminate Native Americans throughout the nineteenth century (and well into the twentieth century) yield a long list of direct military actions as well as the establishment of long-term military surveillance operations within Native American communities.

The first widespread use of what might be considered early modern military intelligence techniques against civilians came with the widespread labor unrest that took place across the United States in the late nineteenth century. The wave of labor strikes that swept across the country in 1877 caused industrialists and big business owners to appeal to the federal government for military intervention. Active-duty federal troops were often deployed, while at the same time, the state militia system was transformed into the National Guard we recognize today during this turbulent time. National Guard troops—military personnel under the command of state authorities unless "federalized" for duty as U.S. Army soldiers—were often used to crush strikes in such far-flung areas as West Virginia, Massachusetts, and Colorado. These interventions often led to violence, such as the 1912 Ludlow Massacre in Colorado, where National Guard troops opened fire on a tent city of strikers and their families using machine guns, then setting the tents on fire. When the smoke cleared, twenty-one people were dead, most of them women and children. Military troops continued to monitor labor activists and meetings through the 1930s.

During this period, there grew a concern that the unfettered use of the military in domestic affairs could very well lead to the sort of tyranny the Founders fought so hard to avoid. Laws were passed to address these concerns, such as the Posse Comitatus Act of 1878, which barred the military from domestic law enforcement, and the Anti-Pinkerton Act of 1893, which limited the president's power to employ private undercover agents. But crises—real and imagined—caused many to ignore these laws, or at least the parts that were seen as inconvenient in troubled times. This is not a new phenomenon, of course. As Oliver Cromwell once said, "Necessity has no law."

The violent strikes of the late nineteenth century, along with a virulent national anti-immigrant sentiment—especially toward southern and eastern Europeans—combined to dampen Americans' fears of a standing internal army by replacing them with fears of an external enemy who was silently infiltrating the country. Labor activists were often portrayed as "foreign communists" or "foreign anarchists," and there was a widespread fear that this foreign element was actively conspiring to bring down the country. Citizens began to warm to the idea that federal troops could somehow protect them from this threat and maintain the current social, political, and economic order. As the United States' entrance into World War I grew imminent, the military began to deploy its growing intelligence infrastructure domestically, despite the existence of laws like the Posse Comitatus Act that restricted such activities. The Army worked closely with citizen-run patriot groups, such as the American Protective League, which was a quasi-military organization created to operate secretly within communities to "ferret[] out spies, slackers, and saboteurs." After a number of Army surveillance scandals were revealed in the 1920s, the military's domestic intelligence apparatus was severely curtailed. But there remained a system of passive civilian surveillance within the Army that soon found new life as another world war loomed.

Army domestic surveillance programs were quickly revived as the United States entered World War II. The Army's Counter Intelligence Corps (CIC) deployed its newly trained special agents to protect critical infrastructure from saboteurs and root out enemies spying from within. As the Cold War took the place of World War II, Army domestic surveillance continued to grow, now with a mission to uncover communist infiltrators, an exercise that quickly expanded to the monitoring of all "subversive" groups and individuals. This poorly—and often subjectively—defined term gave military intelligence groups license to expand their domestic surveillance net to include civil rights groups, student groups, labor organizations, women's rights groups, and religious organizations, as well as leaders and other key individuals within those groups.

The Army's desire for this information was not completely unreasonable. While laws such as the Posse Comitatus Act forbade general military involvement in domestic law enforcement, the law did permit civilian authorities to call on the U.S. military to assist in quelling riots and insurrections, and in other civil emergencies. During the widespread civil unrest of the 1960s, Army troops were frequently called on to assist local and state governments in keeping order. In 1967 and 1968 alone, the National Guard was mobilized eighty-three times and the Army deployed four times to suppress riots in American cities. Army troops were deployed in Washington, D.C., throughout 1969 and 1970 to control Vietnam War protesters. Many of the protest actions took a violent turn, with over five hundred bombings in the United States reported in 1969, a number that doubled for each of the next two years.

The Army clearly needed to establish an effective domestic surveillance program to support these often-dangerous deployments. This was the environment many young military intelligence officers were facing in the 1960s, including a young Army Reserve officer from New England named Christopher Pyle.

When Pyle graduated from Bowdoin College in 1961, he accepted a commission as a U.S. Army Reserve officer.[3] His active duty was put on hold, however, while Pyle attended Columbia University, obtaining an LL.B. from Columbia Law School and a master's degree in public law and government from Columbia in 1966. He reported for duty on August 1 that same year, and began training as an army intelligence officer and counterintelligence agent at the Military Intelligence School at Fort Holabird.

Pyle's first assignment was as an instructor at Fort Holabird, training future Army counterintelligence special agents on investigative legal principles. Among his duties was leading a one-hour course entitled "CONUS Intelligence and Spot Reports," CONUS being the military abbreviation for "Continental United States." The course curriculum was largely made up of the laws authorizing the military to assist civilian authorities to control riots and in other similar emergencies. Pyle focused on the intelligence needs of a riot control unit commander, such as the layout of cities to help plan for troop placement and transportation. The spot reports in question contained a six-paragraph incident report describing an action or event relevant to the military's role in assisting civilian police with riot control. As Pyle discovered, one could not cover much more than this in a mere hour.

There was no curriculum for the course, so Pyle came up with one by asking the basic question, What does the Army need to go into a city in the United States to assist in a civil emergency? Military assistance to civilian authorities was not a concept new to the 1960s. The U.S. military had been backing up local police since the earliest years of the nation, starting with George Washington's call for military assistance to suppress the Whiskey Rebellion in 1794. So Pyle sat down in the Baltimore Library to find everything he could on the history of riots in the United States, and the military's response, if any. The first piece of information that the military would need would be maps—the Army needed to transport troops and equipment, and would need to find suitable roads to do so. This meant finding out the heights of overpasses and bridges to ensure that large trucks could pass beneath them, recording the weight limits of roads, identifying open spaces where troops could base their operations, ensuring water supply points, and so on. These were all very basic—and very dry—requirements to be taught in a one-hour class.

Following one of these classes in early 1968, a young lieutenant approached Pyle and said, "Captain Pyle, you don't know much about this, do you?" Pyle admitted that this was the case, and asked the lieutenant what he could tell him. The lieutenant told Pyle that before coming to his class, he was a special duty officer at the CONUS Intelligence Section of the Army Intelligence Command, and offered to arrange a briefing there for Captain Pyle. Two weeks later, Pyle accompanied the lieutenant to the Army Intelligence Command building, an imposing black edifice once used as a railroad engine assembly plant that had since been converted to Army office space. They were issued special security passes at the door, and were led down through a maze of corridors that finally opened up on a brightly lit room containing a large steel cage. There, Pyle was introduced to Andrew Havre, a civilian, and Major McLay, who together ran the CONUS Intelligence Section. Their briefing lasted only about an hour and fifteen minutes, but during that short time, Pyle's world was forever changed.

As Havre led Pyle through the CONUS Intelligence Section offices, he pointed out the large bank of teletype machines chattering noisily. Havre explained that the teletypes were receiving field reports, submitted in real time across the country by special agents, reporting on any demonstration of twenty people or more. Once these reports were received, analysts would review each one, possibly passing them up to higher headquarters for further actions. Once recorded, each of the incoming field reports was stored in nearby file cabinets. Havre was eager to show Pyle how the section had automated the labor-intensive task of surveillance analysis through the use of cutting-edge computer database technologies, indicating to Pyle a tall stack of computer punch cards. Each of these cards, explained Havre, represented a person or event, which could then be stored and searched using their powerful mainframe computers. Pyle glanced at the top card on the stack and observed that it was a record for Arlo Tatum, then the executive director of the Central Committee for Conscientious Objectors. When Pyle examined the card to see why, exactly, the Army would be interested enough in Tatum to keep records on him, he could find only a notation on the card that stated that Tatum had once given a speech on the legal rights of conscientious objectors at the University of Oklahoma.

Havre next showed Pyle a multivolume set of paperback "mug books," similar to those typically kept by civilian police departments containing photographs of convicted criminals. Havre referred to the CONUS Intelligence Section's version of this mug book as its "blacklist." When Pyle asked what the book was for, Havre replied, "To keep track of people who might cause trouble for the Army." Pyle opened the first volume in the set and saw a picture of Ralph David Abernathy, who was Martin Luther King's assistant with the Southern Christian Leadership Conference. Under Abernathy's photo was a police record. Pyle glanced at the cover of the volume, which bore the title "Persons Active in Civil Disturbances." Pyle replaced the mug book on its shelf.

Before he left, Pyle asked Havre whether he had any materials he could take back to show his students. Havre stepped over to one of the teletype machines and tore off a five-foot-long printout containing a summary of activities for the week of March 11 through March 18, 1968. Pyle skimmed the report and noticed that one of the entries described undercover Army special agents monitoring meetings at a Unitarian church. This was just the sort of activity Pyle told his students to avoid. Pyle later noted that there was nothing sinister in the apparent intentions of the CONUS Intelligence Section personnel he met on his tour of the facility. Despite this observation, however, Pyle became aware that the Army had "assembled the essential apparatus of a police state." He now knew what the young lieutenant had meant when he observed, "Captain Pyle, you don't know much about this, do you?" The lieutenant was right, but Captain Pyle was beginning to learn.

A few weeks after his tour of the CONUS Intelligence Section, Pyle received a call from the speechwriter for General William Blakefield, then the commanding general of Army Intelligence Command. The speechwriter wanted to know whether Pyle had done any research behind the legal basis for the Army's CONUS intelligence program. Indeed, Pyle had done such research, but first asked the speechwriter whether General Blakefield's Judge Advocate General (JAG) officer—essentially, the general's chief counsel—had prepared any research on the topic. The speechwriter replied that no, no memorandum giving a legal basis to the program had ever been written. Pyle then began to outline his findings to the speechwriter, based on his extensive study of U.S. laws regarding the use of military personnel to stop riots, rebellions, and insurrections. Pyle's research showed that the military had the clear authority to gather tactical intelligence about cities, such as road networks, potential equipment staging sites, and other information necessary for the efficient deployment of military units. But, warned Pyle, the law does not authorize the military to go beyond these tactical intelligence-gathering tasks, and certainly did not support the collection of information about the political activities of law-abiding citizens. In fact, Pyle pointed out to the speechwriter that the activities he saw while visiting the CONUS Intelligence Section may well have been unconstitutional.

Finally, Pyle brought up the history of the struggle between the military branches and civilian law enforcement over who had jurisdictional precedence over intelligence activities in the United States. During the first months leading up to the United States' entrance into the Second World War, there was a scramble at the federal level to shore up its flagging intelligence community. In 1939 the Roosevelt administration issued an order that restricted all investigations of espionage and sabotage to the Army, Navy, and FBI. In 1942 these agencies entered into a Delimitations Agreement, which stated that the Army's Military Intelligence Division and the Office of Naval Intelligence would have jurisdiction over all military and civilian personnel of the service branches, and the FBI would oversee all other counterintelligence matters. In 1942 a secret meeting was held between representatives of the Army, Navy, FBI, and FCC—all of which were involved in the wartime intelligence effort—where the question of whether this growing multitude of intelligence offices and activities should be somehow consolidated. As World War II ended and the Cold War began, J. Edgar Hoover's FBI intensified its lobbying for a bigger piece of the intelligence pie. In 1947 President Truman issued Executive Order 9835, which created a Federal Loyalty Program, and gave the FBI jurisdiction over all investigations of civilians. This order conflicted with the 1942 Delimitations Agreement, and prompted negotiations over a replacement. In 1949 the Army and the FBI signed a new Delimitations Agreement, which allowed the FBI to conduct all investigations of civilians (including Army civilians) in the Western

Hemisphere, leaving the remainder of the globe to the Army. Pyle told the speechwriter that the current activities of the CONUS Intelligence Section likely violated the 1949 Delimitations Agreement.

Pyle ended the conversation with the general's speechwriter with a warning: Even if the activities of the CONUS Intelligence Section were technically legal, were ultimately found to be constitutional, and did not violate past agreements regarding the conduct of surveillance of American civilians, the mere existence of such a program would be extremely embarrassing to the Army if it ever became public. The speechwriter thanked Pyle for the information, telling him that he would pass all of it on to the general. Pyle never heard from the speechwriter, or from the general's office, again.

Pyle's active duty commitment came to an end soon after that telephone conversation, and he returned to Columbia University to pursue a PhD. After a year of studies there, Pyle began to think back on what he had seen at the CONUS Intelligence Section, and began to grow concerned that the program might still be running unabated, despite his legal analysis, which may or may not have ever been seen by the commanding general. He started to write down his thoughts on the matter, and it soon began to take the shape of an article. Pyle spent over two months drafting and editing the article, knowing that he had seen only a tiny fraction of the Army's civilian surveillance operations, and did not want his thoughts to be misconstrued or his words used to extrapolate conjecture and speculation. He was a former Army officer, after all. He did not want to attack the Army or the government, but to protect it from itself. Pyle was no radical bomb thrower, and carefully chose every word and sentence in his draft article as an accurate description of what he saw and what he knew only.

The article began to take the form of a position piece. Pyle began with a careful analysis of the laws supporting the use of military units to suppress civilian unrest in extreme cases, which required an intelligence program to prepare for such an action, should it ever become necessary. This intelligence collection would include up-to-date maps of cities, analysis of transportation options, and possible places to load and store equipment. But Pyle quickly pointed out that this intelligence collection did not include the surveillance of law-abiding citizens or the compilation of dossiers on their affiliations and political activities. The article then discussed the possible negative effects on the Army, the government, and the country if the CONUS Intelligence Section's program was allowed to continue. Pyle finished the article by recommending a number of steps that could be taken by each of the three branches of government to put legal limits on the program without necessarily closing the section down entirely. Pyle's goal was to make sure the program was legal, not to eliminate it. When he was finally satisfied with the article, he submitted it to the *Washington Monthly* for consideration. It published Pyle's article, titled "CONUS Intelligence: The Army Watches Civilian Politics," in January 1970.

Pyle was not at all sure what kind of reaction his article would get. Political tensions were running very high at the time—including widespread protests against the war in Vietnam, struggles for racial equality, and political assassinations—and the federal government under President Richard Nixon was circling the wagons. The Nixon administration could play dirty. One particular method the Nixon White House found useful was to "screw" with political enemies through IRS tax audits, manipulation of grant availability and federal contracts, litigation, or prosecution—whatever tools the executive branch could bring to bear. The Nixon administration went so far as to formalize this process through what became known as Nixon's Enemies List, a memorandum compiled and updated by Nixon's staff to keep track of people Nixon did not like, and ensure that they were dealt with accordingly. Perhaps unsurprisingly, Pyle ended up on this list for his article, receiving a notice that he was the subject of an IRS audit soon after publication. It turned out, however, that the auditors discovered that Pyle's wife had overpaid her taxes by $154, so the Treasury Department had to issue Pyle a refund check—an unexpected windfall, courtesy of Nixon's Enemies List.

Not all of the responses to the article were negative, however. Soon after publication, Pyle began to receive calls and letters from former Army intelligence agents who were asking some of the same questions Pyle had. Most of these former agents requested anonymity, fearing the sort of backlash they knew the Nixon administration was capable of. These former agents all emphasized their belief that they, and the other Army personnel they worked with, did not have any sort of sinister motives, but were stuck feeding a nationwide surveillance system that had taken on a life of its own. Pyle knew exactly what these former agents were talking about, and was deeply appreciative of their offers of help. He knew that his little article was not going to be enough to change the system, but it could act as that first pebble in an avalanche of information that might expose Army civilian surveillance programs to sunlight.

In the months following his article's publication, former Army intelligence agents began to tell Pyle about other civilian computerized data collection programs across the military. In addition, every military intelligence group headquarters, along with all of their subordinate regional offices, field offices, and resident offices, kept extensive paper files on civilian organizations and individuals. One agent told Pyle of a separate civilian surveillance program being run by the Continental Army Command (CONARC), controlling nine Army divisions, three separate brigades, two armored cavalry regiments, thirty-seven support brigades, and a range of other support units. The Army's civilian surveillance programs were clearly much larger and more complex than Pyle could have imagined.

The Continental Army Command was the Army organization in charge of nearly all Army units in the continental United States at the time. Along with the Army Intelligence Command, which employed about 1,200 plainclothes special agents deployed around the country, these military agencies operated an enormous intelligence collection apparatus, often in direct competition with one another as well as with civilian law enforcement agencies, the FBI, and the U.S. Secret Service. When these groups were not competing, they would share intelligence information with one another—Army intelligence agents often relied heavily on the FBI for much of their information. Information collected by Army special agents would then be distributed throughout the military, with direct intelligence feeds to the Pentagon, Army riot control units, and every U.S. Army command around the world, many of which had no apparent need for information about civil disturbances in the United States.

As Pyle saw during his visit to the CONUS Intelligence Section at Fort Holabird, these Army intelligence units were all collecting data on U.S. citizens, building dossiers containing computer punch card files, photographs, and newspaper clippings on individuals and organizations. One card file sent to him by a former Army special agent came from the 113th Military Intelligence Group, with headquarters in Minneapolis. The file's title indicated that it contained information for a two-month period in 1968. When Pyle read the file, he was shocked by the detailed information Army special agents had gathered about ordinary citizens. Some examples of the file's entries included the following:

- James Griffin. St. Paul Department of Human Rights. 8 January '68. Teach-in draws crowd with speeches, seminar.
- Scott Halazon. University of Colorado graduate student. 26 April '68. Strike organizers hope 5,000 will skip class. 24 April '68. Faculty, students to strike Friday.
- Jane Hanger. YMCA employee. 1 May '68. Teach-in to examine white racism in U.S.
- E. Johnson. (UM Student Mobilization Committee). 9 May '68. Speaker SMC meeting.

Pyle saw that the file was filled with such entries, and also included photographs, some taken at events, others from local police files or newspaper stories. He could see that the military domestic surveillance infrastructure was quietly growing out of control, with no real public oversight.

After the publication of Pyle's article, however, the public began to take notice, and the Army went on the defensive.[4] Congress began to make inquiries, both the House of Representatives and the Senate made preparations for formal inquiries, and Army leadership was feeling cornered. The Pentagon's first reaction was to stay mum on the topic. When asked by reporters and members of Congress about the allegations in Pyle's article, the Pentagon's Office of Public Information refused to comment, and directed journalists to submit all of their questions regarding the CONUS intelligence program in writing. Behind this façade, however, the Army was scrambling. The Army's military intelligence headquarters at Fort Holabird sent urgent messages to each of its subordinate intelligence groups, instructing them to collect only "essential elements of information." Intelligence special agents were ordered not to talk to any journalists about the domestic surveillance program. Any agent caught doing so would be immediately prosecuted for breaching national security. The Army's general counsel, Robert E. Jordan III, quickly halted all responses to congressional questions, going so far as to refuse receipt of such inquiries.

In the face of this widespread—and growing—criticism, however, the Army had to do something, so it began to focus on the optics. On January 26, 1970, Army leadership admitted, in a series of statements, that the CONUS intelligence collection program did, in fact, exist. The problem with these admissions, however, was in their use of half-truths to mask omissions or outright falsehoods. For example, while the Army acknowledged the existence of the CONUS intelligence program, it also claimed that any political intelligence it happened to collect was only "in connection with Army civil disturbance responsibilities." Based on the large quantities of evidence Pyle had been receiving from former Army special agents since his article's publication, he knew this to be false. The Army also admitted to passing its special agents' spot reports around the world via its automated teletype network, and placing this information in a computer database using a punch card system, but followed this statement with the assertion that "this is incident information only and does not include individual biographies or personality data." Pyle knew this to be false as well.

Pyle was not the only one to be unimpressed by the Army's early responses. Members of Congress from across the political spectrum began to send direct inquiries to the secretary of the Army. Senator Sam Ervin, a member of the Senate Armed Services Committee and a former judge, stated, "The Army has no business operating data banks for the surveillance of private citizens; nor do they have any business in domestic politics."[5] Throughout the month of February 1970, however, the Army continued to stonewall Congress, while at the same time conducting its own internal investigation, dispatching Robert Jordan to Fort Holabird to personally assess the program.[6] While there, Jordan was shocked to discover that the CONUS Intelligence Section's "dissidents" database contained a lengthy and detailed report on Coretta Scott King, Martin Luther King's wife. Finally, on February 26, Jordan sent a letter to members of Congress containing an extensive defense of the Army's collection of files on individuals applying for security clearances. This was never a contested program, however, and was yet another red herring. Following this defense, the letter closed with the following: "There have been some activities which have been undertaken in the civil disturbance field which, on review, have been determined to be beyond the Army's mission requirements." Jordan's letter then gave a brief itemization of examples of such activities, including the Intelligence Command's publication of "an identification list which included the names and descriptions of individuals who might become involved in civil disturbance situations," and "a computer data bank" operated by the Intelligence Command, which "included information about potential incidents and individuals involved in potential civil disturbance incidents." Jordan assured the members of Congress that the "identification list" and the "data bank" had been ordered to be destroyed.

Jordan's assurances, however, were incomplete, and failed to mention a number of other Army domestic surveillance programs, all of which were currently operating. These programs included a two-volume encyclopedia titled *Counterintelligence Research Project: Cities and Organizations of Interest and Individuals of Interest*, which contained information on the Urban League, the John Birch Society, and the Fifth Avenue Peace Parade Committee as well as individuals such as the playwright LeRoi Jones and Martin Luther King; a microfilm archive of political protests and civil disturbances, containing information on the Southern Christian Leadership Conference, Young Americans for Freedom, and the Center for the Study of Democratic Institutions as well as individuals such as Navy Rear Admiral Arnold E. True and Brigadier General Hugh B. Tester (both critics of the war in Vietnam), Georgia state representative Julian Bond, and singers Joan Baez and Arlo Guthrie; a computerized data bank on civil disturbances, political protests, and "resistance in the Army"; regional data banks at each Army command; and large collections of files at most of the Intelligence Command's three hundred CONUS offices.

Congressional responses to Jordan's letter were mixed. Some were pleased with the assurances and were clearly eager to move past this issue. Congressman Cornelius Gallagher, a Democrat from New Jersey and chair of the House Invasion of Privacy Subcommittee, while aware of the many omissions in Jordan's letter, assured the press that the Army would no longer engage in domestic political surveillance of groups and individuals. The *New York Times* published Gallagher's statement in an article titled "Army Ends Watch on Civil Protests." Senator Ervin, however, was not satisfied by the Jordan letter, and renewed his demand for a full congressional investigation, stating, "If there ever were a case of military overkill, this is it. . . . Under our Constitution [the] enemy is not the American citizen."[7] Ervin specifically questioned Jordan's failure to address many of the intelligence files identified by Pyle in his article.

On March 20, Secretary of the Army Thaddeus Beal wrote to both Ervin and Gallagher, asserting that "[t]he only 'intelligence files' concerning civilians maintained by the Army consist of the files maintained by the Counterintelligence Analysis Division."[8] But Beal's letter also failed to mention the CONARC computer files, the Intelligence Command's regional data banks, or the files maintained by intelligence sections of the U.S.-based Army commands. Despite these omissions, Beal assured the members of Congress that no new computerized data banks would be established without the approval of the secretary of the Army and the chief of staff following "consultations with concerned committees of Congress." Gallagher was satisfied with Beal's letter, but Senator Ervin was not.[9] Ervin considered calling the Senate Judiciary Subcommittee on Constitutional Rights into session, but the committee members' calendars were full, so a complete congressional investigation of the Army's domestic surveillance program would have to wait. Meanwhile, a few blocks away from the Capitol Building, a group of individuals was taking the challenge to Army domestic surveillance to another venue—the U.S. courts.

Getting through the Courthouse Door

In 1948 Arlo Tatum, then twenty-five years old, was facing time in a federal prison for the second time in his young life. On both occasions, Tatum's crime had been one not of violence, but of nonviolence. Born to a Quaker family in West Branch, Iowa, in 1923, Tatum had been strictly opposed to war and government conscription since he first considered these issues as a child.[1] At fourteen, Tatum wrote a dramatic poem after seeing the family's clothesline pole, visible from his bedroom window, as a cross, a symbol of conscription programs for military service. His absolutist Quaker beliefs on these topics were given their first real test when he was eighteen years old and working in a Quaker community in Mexico.

In September 1940, after considerable debate, Congress passed the Burke-Wadsworth Selective Training and Service Act, which required all men between the ages of twenty-one and thirty-five to register with their local draft boards. Once signed into law by Franklin Roosevelt, the Burke-Wadsworth Act became the first peacetime conscription program in U.S. history. European politics had been anything but stable following the signing of the Treaty of Versailles, the 1919 peace agreement that ended the First World War by setting the stage for the next one. In Russia, Italy, Spain, and Germany, things steadily deteriorated through the 1920s and 1930s, while on the other side of the world, Japan was building an empire in Asia. The growing militarism across the globe led many within the U.S. military and political leadership to see the writing on the wall, spurring a rapid buildup of army and naval forces that had been downsized in the years following the 1918 ceasefire.

Following the December 1941 attack on the U.S. naval base at Pearl Harbor by Japanese Imperial forces, the Selective Service Act was altered to raise the maximum age of registration to sixty-five and the minimum age to eighteen. With this change, Tatum was now required to register with his local draft board in Iowa. Conflicted over his objection to conscription and war, he ultimately decided not to avoid the draft by remaining in Mexico, but instead returned to the United States to seek advice on his options as a pacifist in a country now eager for a shot at revenge against the Japanese and, by proxy, Germany and Italy, the other Axis powers. Tatum sought counsel with the American Friends Service Committee in Philadelphia, a Quaker social justice organization founded in 1917 to assist civilian victims of World War I. He did not get the answer he wanted. For three days, organizers at AFSC tried to convince Tatum to comply with the law and register under Section 5(g) of the Selective Service Act, which provided for exemptions from combat service for conscientious objectors.

Tatum's objections to conscription were so strong, however, that any form of registration—even as a conscientious objector—was unacceptable to him. He made an appointment to see Dr. Evan Thomas, then chair of the War Resisters League in New York. Founded in 1923 by people who had opposed World War I, the WRL was part of the larger War Resisters' International, based in London. Thomas was no stranger to the active opposition to militarism, having spent time in prison for his own refusal to enter the military during World War I. After prison, Thomas went back to school, became a medical doctor, and joined the WRL in the late 1930s. The contrarian genes seemed to run in the Thomas family: Evan's brother, Norman, was one of the founders of the American Civil Liberties Union and was the American Socialist Party's candidate for president in 1940. Tatum was well aware of Thomas's background, and he went in to the meeting quite confident that he would soon have a solution that would serve his conscience. Tatum explained to Thomas that he could not register with his draft board under any circumstances. He was quite shocked when Thomas said, "Young man, I advise you to register." Tatum immediately made to leave the office, but Thomas, seeing the pain in Tatum's face, asked him to sit back down to talk about his options. They decided that Tatum would write a letter to U.S. Attorney General Francis Biddle explaining his intentions not to register.

It is worth noting just how difficult—and dangerous—it was to speak, let alone act, against the draft after December 7, 1941. One horrifying example of the very real danger of dissent during this period can be found in the treatment of Jehovah's Witnesses, who opposed all war and refused to salute the flag of any nation. This made them targets of remorseless vigilantism; by the end of World War II, more than 1,600 Jehovah's Witnesses were beaten, tarred and feathered, tortured, castrated, or killed.[2] In most of these cases, local law enforcement agencies refused to intervene, and on a few occasions, even took part.

Prior to the Japanese attack on Pearl Harbor, Americans were ambivalent about getting involved in another costly war that did not appear to involve them. American isolationist tendencies bloomed in the years following World War I, leaning heavily toward non-interventionism even during the Japanese invasion of Manchuria, the Italian conquest of Ethiopia, the Spanish Civil War, and the German annexation of Austria and invasion of Poland. Attitudes began to change in 1940, when France succumbed to the overwhelming German onslaught, and the United States once again expanded its military, and began providing Lend-Lease aid to the Soviet Union, Great Britain, and China. After Pearl Harbor, Americans rushed to support the war effort, flooding enlistment offices, eager for a chance to see combat against Japanese, German, or Italian troops. These newly minted war boosters had little patience for dissenting voices in this effort, all of whom were suspect as, at best, unpatriotic, and at worst, criminally disloyal. Even those who were historically known as stalwart defenders of civil liberties began to rethink those positions in 1941.[3]

Attorney General Francis Biddle fell into this camp. A New Deal Democrat, Biddle was tapped by President Roosevelt to lead the National Labor Relations Board, and served in his Roosevelt's administration as solicitor general and attorney general. His passion for civil liberties led to his later appointments as head of the ACLU and Americans for Democratic Action, and he published multiple books and papers defending the civil rights of all Americans, especially the constitutionally protected right of free speech. Even in mid-1941, as the entry of the United States into the war raging in Europe began to look more and more like a foregone conclusion, Biddle asserted, "We do not lose our right to condemn either measures or men because the country is at war,"[4] and promised that the country would "not again fall into the disgraceful hysteria of witch hunts . . . which were such a dark chapter in our record of the last World War."[5] Immediately following Biddle's appointment as attorney general, Roosevelt took him aside to convince him that it was necessary to take a more pragmatic approach to civil liberties in order to "deal with the subversive element."[6] Biddle reluctantly softened his tone on civil liberties, and ultimately acceded to pressure from both the White House and the public to initiate more than 300,000 investigations and prosecutions of treason, espionage, sabotage, and sedition in 1942 alone, about many of which Biddle would later express his regret.

All of this speaks to the overwhelming feeling of national existential dread—and attendant bellicosity—most Americans felt after the Japanese attack on Pearl Harbor, when even ardent civil liberties defenders like Biddle could be persuaded to begin suspending some of those rights, and those opposed to the war risked physical harm if their views became known. This was the environment in which Arlo Tatum elected to let the attorney general know that he would not be registering for the draft under any circumstances. After sending his letter, Tatum thanked Evan Thomas and went back to his parents' home in Iowa to await his fate.

He did not have to wait long. As it happened, the federal marshal in Tatum's small town was a family friend, often playing bridge with Tatum's parents. On the day Arlo was to be arrested, the marshal knocked on the Tatums' door with tears in his eyes. When Arlo's mother answered the door, the only words the marshal was able to speak were "I've come to take Arlo." The unusual and tragic circumstances were not enough, however, to dampen midwestern Quaker social graces. The marshal was offered coffee by Mrs. Tatum, and they sat together for a while before Arlo was taken to the county jail in Humboldt. After answering the charges with a guilty plea, he was sent to the federal prison at Sandstone, Minnesota, to serve his two-year sentence. The draft ended on March 31, 1947.

As Cold War tensions began to grow after the end of World War II, President Truman signed the Selective Service Act of 1948, which required all American men aged eighteen and older to register with the Selective Service, and brought back draft eligibility for all men between the ages of nineteen and twenty-six. When the new law went into effect, Arlo happened to be touring Canada with his singing group. Friends urged him to stay in Canada. Arlo, who was nearly twenty-six at the time, knew that even if he did register, by the time the administrative paperwork was complete, he would no longer be eligible for the draft under the new system. His conscience, however, would not allow him to either remain in Canada or register with the Selective Service, and Arlo was once again arrested when he returned to the United States. He entered his guilty plea, and was sentenced to serve two years at the Medical Center for Federal Prisoners in Springfield, Missouri.

Two stints in federal prison did nothing to dampen Tatum's convictions. He later reflected that he had not wasted his time in prison, and in fact many people managed to waste more of their time in universities and offices; it was important to grow through any experience. Further, Tatum felt that taking one of the easier roads that would have kept him out of prison would have meant that he was not willing to accept the consequences of his total rejection of conscription, and he would therefore not have the moral standing to help lead the peace movement. Upon his release in 1950, he immediately continued his life's work of singing, advocating nonviolence, protesting militarization, and opposing the draft.

This life was nearly cut short in 1951, when Tatum was seriously injured when a train collided with his car. He was rushed to the hospital, where doctors there did not expect him to survive long. After months of painful recovery and rehabilitation, however, Tatum once again jumped back on his life's path, becoming co-executive secretary of the War Resisters League and, in 1955, moving to London to become general secretary of War Resisters' International. While there, Tatum was also director of Peace News and helped found the World Peace Brigade. Tatum also met his wife, Polly, while in England, and together they returned to Philadelphia, where he was appointed executive secretary of the Central Committee for Conscientious Objectors (CCCO) in 1961.

It was in this capacity that Tatum joined with others to challenge the U.S. Army's domestic surveillance programs. Following Christopher Pyle's revelations of domestic military intelligence programs, Tatum, through the CCCO, and his fellow plaintiffs filed a complaint in the United States District Court for the District of Columbia on February 17, 1970, naming Secretary of Defense Melvin R. Laird and several senior Army officials as defendants.[7] The *Tatum* complaint alleged that the Army's domestic surveillance programs had chilled activities that were otherwise protected under the First Amendment, were outside the scope of activities allowed to the military by law, and, even if seen as part of the Army's lawful duties to protect the nation, far exceeded the needs of any such constitutional or statutory role of the military with respect to civilian activities. Tatum and the other plaintiffs sought a declaration from the court that the Army's surveillance activities were unconstitutional, as well as preliminary and permanent injunctions restraining the Army from engaging in the sort of military intelligence surveillance of civilian activities as revealed by Pyle.

The Army responded by arguing that its legal role of maintaining order in the event of civil disturbances required exactly the sort of military intelligence collection activities the plaintiffs listed in their complaint. While holding that the details of these activities must be kept secret for operational reasons, the defendants urged the court to hold that the conduct described was indeed constitutional, and the complaint should be dismissed for failure to state claims upon which relief can be granted.

The Federal Rules of Civil Procedure (FRCP), the rules created by the Supreme Court for the governance of all civil actions and proceedings before U.S. federal courts, establishes a number of procedural "hoops" through which parties seeking relief must jump before their case will be heard. These procedural filters are there to ensure the "just, speedy, and inexpensive determination of every action and proceeding" before federal courts. (How well these rules accomplish these tasks remains an item for debate to this day.) FRCP Rule 12(b)(6) allows defendants to submit pretrial motions to the court asking for dismissal of the case based solely on the content of the plaintiff's complaint. The origins of this rule can be found in the common law pleading of *demurrer*, where a defendant points out to the court that the plaintiff's complaint—even if accepted as true—contains no valid *causes of action* (another legal term of art) upon which the court is allowed to rule. Rule 12(b)(6) codified this approach to allow federal courts to dismiss insubstantial or frivolous claims at an early stage in the process, before the expensive stages of evidence discovery and trial take place.[8]

The district court judge assigned to hear the *Tatum* case was George L. Hart Jr. Born in Roanoke, Virginia, in 1905, and graduating from Harvard Law School in 1930, Hart practiced law in Washington, D.C., until the United States declared war on Japan, whereupon he entered the Army as an artillery captain, eventually rising to the rank of colonel. In 1958 President Eisenhower offered Hart a recess appointment seat on the U.S. District Court for the District of Columbia, a position for which Hart was confirmed in 1959. He quickly established a reputation as an "outspoken conservative with impeccable Republican credentials and a well-established dislike for protesters," who was quite unafraid to assess stiff sentences in his court.[9] Any hearing before Judge Hart that questioned the authority of government was bound to be an uphill climb for the plaintiffs.

Oral arguments on the pretrial motions before the court in the *Tatum* case were scheduled for April 22, 1970. The plaintiffs, knowing that it would be difficult to convince Judge Hart both that their claims had merit and that these claims were enough to warrant a preliminary injunction against the Army, brought with them a number of former Army military intelligence agents who were prepared to provide sworn testimony on behalf of the plaintiffs as to the scope and nature of Army domestic surveillance activities. Plaintiffs' counsel had not managed to obtain affidavits from these witnesses, however. When the plaintiffs asked to present their witnesses during oral argument, Hart refused, stating that oral argument by counsel only would suffice. One of the plaintiffs' attorneys, Professor Frank Askin of the Rutgers University School of Law, again asked the court to hear the witnesses' testimony, as they were present in the courtroom and were able to testify about the existence of Army domestic surveillance. Hart ignored Askin's plea, and concluded that the activities complained of by the plaintiffs in this cases amounted to no more than the clipping of news media reports, which was perfectly legal under the Constitution. Hart then ruled from the bench in favor of the defendants, disposing of the plaintiffs' case under FRCP Rule 12(b)(6).

The *Tatum* plaintiffs didn't want to wait for Hart's written order—which would not be issued until April 29—to appeal his ruling. On April 23 the plaintiffs filed an appeal with the Court of Appeals for the District of Columbia. Oral argument was heard on January 20, 1971, and on April 27, just over a year after Hart's dismissal of the plaintiffs' case, the appeals court issued its opinion reversing the lower court's ruling, remanding the case back to Hart with specific directions. Judge Malcolm Richard Wilkey, writing the majority opinion for the court of appeals, acknowledged the legitimate needs of the military to maintain a certain level of information in order to fulfill its duty to quell civil disorders.[10] But he added that the real questions were "what type of information the military needs, how they should go about obtaining it, when they need it, and whether what the Army has done here has infringed any of the appellants' rights." Because the trial court had refused to hear testimony at oral argument, Wilkey observed, the court was left with a limited view of the issues, disagreeing with Hart's conclusion that the Army's activities were no different than a newspaper's collection and storage of clippings. Wilkey made it clear that the collection of press clippings by a civilian organization was much different, from a civil liberties point of view, than "such action by the military is."

Wilkey stated that the "evil alleged" by the plaintiffs was that of government "overbreadth," and because this case was a good opportunity to "test the constitutionality of the Army's action," the issues brought by the plaintiffs should be considered justiciable. The court of appeals ordered the case to be reheard by Judge Hart, specifically to determine four key points:

1. The nature of the Army domestic intelligence system that is the subject of appellants' complaint, specifically the extent of the system, the methods of gathering the information, its content and substance, the methods of retention and distribution, and the recipients of the information;
2. What part, if any, of the Army domestic intelligence-gathering system is unrelated to or not reasonably necessary to the performance of the mission as defined by the Constitution, statutes, and military regulations, and as interpreted by actions under those written definitions of the mission;
3. Whether the existence of any overbroad aspects of the intelligence-gathering system, as determined above, has or might have an inhibiting effect on appellants or others similarly situated; and
4. Such relief as called for in accordance with the above established law and facts.

Appeals court judge George MacKinnon disagreed with the majority, and in his dissent, cited the plaintiffs' own oral argument before the trial court:

Our Plaintiffs this morning, for example, are *not people, obviously, who are cowed and chilled*; they've come into Court, but they have to represent millions of Americans not nearly as forward, as courageous, as willing as them to open themselves up to public investigation and public scrutiny. We're not—you know, every citizen is not a Tom Payne [sic]; they're few and far between. (emphasis in original)

Judge MacKinnon took these words to mean that the government activities the plaintiffs complained of "did not cause any substantial infringement of the constitutional rights," which therefore undermined their entire case. He observed in his dissent that "the [alleged] chill to this amorphous group . . . is grounded in the unrealistic and speculative fear that the Government will improperly use the information against them," and noted that the plaintiffs made no "claims that any of the information gathered by the Army has been used in a manner that has injured plaintiffs or imposed on them any penalty attributable to their exercise of their First Amendment rights." In an observation that would come up time and again for plaintiffs seeking to challenge government surveillance programs, MacKinnon stated, "Such indefinite claims of highly visionary apprehensions that are admittedly based on abstractions which cannot be comprehended . . . do not present a case involving facts of sufficient realism and definiteness to confer jurisdiction on the court to make a sweeping constitutional decision affecting important activities of the federal Government." In short, MacKinnon was of the opinion that the *Tatum* plaintiffs lacked standing. He was in the minority, however, and the *Tatum* case was sent back to the lower court to be reheard by Judge Hart. This time, it was the government that disagreed with the court's analysis in its opinion, and it decided to appeal the D.C. Circuit Court's opinion to the Supreme Court. But persuading the Supreme Court to hear your case is not a straightforward matter, and the explanation for this requires a bit of constitutional history.

When the U.S. Supreme Court was created via Article III of the U.S. Constitution, Congress expressly articulated a list of "cases and controversies" that would be decided by the Court. In the famous case of *Marbury v. Madison*, the Court further held that Congress has no constitutional power to extend the Court's original jurisdiction—cases that the Court may hear directly, rather than as an appeal from a lower court— beyond this list.[11] The Court's *appellate* jurisdiction, however, was another matter. The Court's ability to hear appeals from lower courts was subject to the congressional power to make regulations and exceptions, as was made explicit in Section 2 of Article III. This meant that so long as Congress did not make any changes to the constitutional list of cases or controversies the Court was allowed to hear, Congress was free to define the Court's jurisdiction, requiring the Court to hear some cases, while prohibiting the Court from deciding others.[12]

The only court defined by the Constitution was the Supreme Court, and it was not until the Judiciary Act of 1789 was passed that the federal court system we now know began to take shape. Among the powers granted by the act was the ability for all federal courts to issue all writs (a term from English common law meaning a formal, written administrative or judicial order) "necessary or appropriate in aid of their respective jurisdictions and agreeable to the usages and principles of law." One of these allowed writs was the writ of certiorari, a tool used by England's King's Bench to give it jurisdictional control over lower courts. Unlike the English example, however, the Judiciary Act did not give federal courts the ability to use writs to assert jurisdiction, thus limiting the Supreme Court's power to control which cases it heard. The effects of this policy were minimal during the late eighteenth and early nineteenth centuries, when there were relatively few cases to be heard, but by the 1880s, the Court had hundreds of cases on its docket that it simply could not administratively handle, and by 1888, the court had a three-year backlog of cases on its docket.

In 1891 Congress sought to alleviate this problem by creating a layer of intermediate appellate courts between district courts and the Supreme Court, the circuit courts of appeals, giving the Supreme Court mandatory appellate jurisdiction over most of the circuit court decisions, with the remainder to be left as final. But even for these "final" decisions, Congress gave the Supreme Court appellate jurisdiction if the lower court of appeals certified novel, difficult, or important questions of law or if the Supreme Court issued a writ of certiorari to review the lower court's decision. The inclusion of the writ of certiorari power in the 1891 act was driven at least in part by a deep concern in Congress that the intermediate courts of appeals would issue a "diversity of judgments" that were "careless or inadvertent disposition[s] of important litigation by these courts," where certiorari would give "flexibility, elasticity, and openness for supervision by the Supreme Court."[13] The Circuit Court of

Appeals Act of 1891 was passed in the closing days of the 51st Congress, giving the Supreme Court its first real discretionary power to review the judgments of lower courts.

In 1912 William Howard Taft lost his bid for presidential reelection, and began turning his attention to the federal judiciary. It had been something of an open secret that Taft would have much rather been chief justice of the Supreme Court than president, but his wife preferred the latter. Taft had hoped than then-Chief Justice Melville Fuller would resign before the 1908 elections, but when that did not happen, he sought the presidency and was elected. When Fuller died in 1910, Taft was forced to promote Justice Edward Douglass White to the office he had long coveted. But White seemed an odd choice for chief justice. It did not go unnoticed that Taft, a Republican, elevated White, a lifelong Democrat. The elevation of a sitting justice to the office of chief justice was also unusual, a move that had not been made since 1795. White was, however, sixty-five years old and quite overweight at the time of his elevation to chief justice, leading many to conclude that Taft's choice of White was a move calculated to minimize the time White would occupy the office, and maximize the chances that Taft would later be appointed. Taft's strategy ultimately paid off when White died in 1921, and Taft was appointed the next chief justice of the Supreme Court.

Taft's focus on the Supreme Court was also quite political. Taft was disturbed by the rising Progressive movement of the early twentieth century, especially its disposition to entertain social experiments, making it a serious source of popular unrest and a threat to property rights. He saw progressives' use of federal courts as a big part of this problem, and began advocating for judicial reform to limit the influence of progressives and labor unions. Specifically, Taft sought to give the Supreme Court the ability to exercise its own discretion in taking any lower court case "so that it may exercise absolute and arbitrary discretion with respect to all business but constitutional business," which Taft saw as the Court's "most important function."[14] While not particularly effective as president, Taft excelled in the world of judicial politics. He knew that the country was tiring of the rapid changes brought about by a combination of progressivism and World War I, and he began drafting a bill to reform the Supreme Court as a return to "normalcy." Taft began lobbying Congress on behalf of his bill, handpicking senators and representatives to serve on its committees. Key among the reforms in Taft's proposed bill was an expansion of the Supreme Court's certiorari powers. In effect, under Taft's proposed bill, no one would be entitled to Supreme Court review of a lower court's judgment. That decision would be made by the Supreme Court alone through its certiorari power.

Among the key issues debated during the 1924 election was the power of the federal judiciary. The progressive wing of the Republican Party tried to get the party to adopt a platform that would install term limits for federal judges and reject the expansion of judicial powers sought in Taft's proposed bill. Calvin Coolidge, the Republican nominee, rejected this proposal, and portrayed its adherents as dangerous radicals. With Coolidge's election, Taft redoubled his efforts to get his judicial reform bill passed, making multiple visits to the White House and the Capitol Building in support of his cause. His tireless lobbying eventually succeeded, and a largely unmodified version of his bill was eventually passed as the Judiciary Act of 1925, with Congress giving a surprising amount of deference to the Court. Not long after the act was passed, the Supreme Court asserted that its authority to grant certiorari could be limited (by the Court itself) to a particular issue in a case, and ignoring the rest. For example, in the famous government wiretapping case of *Olmstead v. United States*, Taft's majority opinion assumed the authority of the Court to limit the review of the case to constitutional questions only, and ignoring any possible nonconstitutional grounds for the lower court's decision.[15]

Today, the Supreme Court practice of limited grants of certiorari has become an accepted part of the Court's procedures. In fact, this practice has been codified within the Supreme Court Rules, which state that no writ of certiorari will bring all questions in a case before the court, as certiorari once did under the Judiciary Act of 1891. Rather, "[o]nly the questions set out in the petition, or fairly included therein, will be considered by the Court."[16] The Court has clarified this rule as serving its interest by "forc[ing] the parties to focus on the questions the Court has viewed as particularly important."[17] In other words, the Supreme Court does not so much grant certiorari to certain cases, but rather to certain questions. The Court has even gone so far as to grant certiorari and then rewrite the questions presented.

For the government defendants in *Tatum*, the Supreme Court's now well-established policy of limited certiorari meant that they had to demonstrate to the Court that an important legal question not only existed in their case, but also had either not yet been answered by the lower court or had been addressed in a way that was in conflict with other standing court opinions. The government asked for, and received, an extension of time from the Supreme Court to file its petition for a writ of certiorari in its case. On August 25, 1971, the government defendants filed their petition with the Court, requesting review of the following question:

> Whether respondents' claim—that the mere existence of a civil disturbance intelligence system within the Department of the Army generates a chilling effect on the exercise, by persons other than plaintiffs, of First Amendment rights—is justiciable, and is one that these respondents have standing to raise.

The defendants' question was actually two questions cleverly presented in one package. The first question was one of justiciability, asking the Court to decide whether the facts presented in the case rise to the level required by FRCP 12(b)(6). The second question, however, was the one with real bite: Even if the facts in this case presented a justiciable issue, could the plaintiffs bring it before a federal court? In other words, the government was asking the Court to go directly to the issue of plaintiffs' standing in this case based solely on the trial court record as it currently existed, and not on additional testimony and evidence to be gathered at a future trial court hearing, as the court of appeals had requested. The Supreme Court granted the government defendants' petition for a writ of certiorari on November 16, 1971, and oral arguments were later scheduled for March 27, 1972.

As the parties began preparing their respective arguments for briefing before the Supreme Court, four relevant issues loomed large in the background. First, when the *Tatum* plaintiffs filed their original complaint with the D.C. District Court in early 1970, they had based their case upon a somewhat flimsy evidentiary foundation. The evidence the plaintiffs presented to the trial court was based on the data available at the time, which mainly consisted of the facts contained in Christopher Pyle's 1970 *Washington Monthly* article. All that was known at that time was that the U.S. Army had been collecting intelligence data on civilians using public sources. The *Tatum* plaintiffs were prepared to offer additional witness testimony, but the trial court refused to hear them. By the time the case had reached the court of appeals in 1971, much more evidence supporting the plaintiffs' case had emerged, primarily through Senator Ervin's Constitutional Rights Subcommittee hearings, which began proceedings in the first session of the 92nd Congress in 1971.

The problem for the *Tatum* plaintiffs, however, was that while this additional information now existed in the public record, it was not in the trial court record. When Judge Hart examined the evidence before him during the original trial court hearing, it appeared to him that the Army's actions, while possibly inept and a waste of taxpayer funds, were effectively harmless, and therefore nonjusticiable. When the court of appeals heard the case, however, the details of the Ervin hearings and their fallout had been in the press for nearly a year, and two of the three appeals court judges empathized with the plaintiffs with this new factual background. But the dissenting judge pointed out that their opinion should only be "based on the facts of the case which emerge from the pleadings, affidavits and the admissions made to the trial court," and not evidence that was not in the original record. Had the *Tatum* plaintiffs made a mistake in bringing their case too early?

Second, while the *Tatum* case was making its way through the federal courts, a new justice had been appointed to the Supreme Court. When Justice John Harlan retired in September 1971, President Nixon appointed William Rehnquist, then an assistant attorney general in the Justice Department's Office of Legal Counsel, to replace him. Rehnquist was confirmed by the Senate in December, and took his seat on the bench on January 7, 1972. What made this appointment especially relevant to the *Tatum* case was Rehnquist's 1971 appearances, in his capacity as assistant attorney general, before the Ervin Committee to testify as to the Justice Department's role in military intelligence surveillance of U.S. civilians. During these hearings, he gave detailed testimony regarding the legality of these programs and even directly gave his views on the *Tatum* case, which was then before the D.C. Circuit Court of Appeals. When Senator Ervin challenged Rehnquist's September 20, 1971, memorandum of law defending the government activities described in *Tatum* as constitutional, Rehnquist stated,

My only point of disagreement with you is to say whether as in the case of *Tatum v. Laird* that has been pending in the Court of Appeals here in the District of Columbia that an action will lie by private citizens to enjoin the gathering of information by the executive branch where there has been no threat of compulsory process and no pending action against any of those individuals on the part of the government.

Rehnquist thus publicly made his position quite clear: The *Tatum* plaintiffs did not have standing to bring their challenge to government surveillance programs before federal courts.

Rehnquist's presence on the Supreme Court thus created a potential impartiality problem in the *Tatum* case. The Court has long emphasized the importance of maintaining an impartial forum for litigants, which may sometimes require that a judge be disqualified from hearing a particular case. In fact, if there is any basis for recusal whatsoever, the judge must not hesitate to recuse himself or herself from the proceedings in order to "avoid even the appearance of bias."[18] Even though such a regime "may sometimes bar trial by judges who have no actual bias and who would do their very best to weigh the scales of justice equally between contending parties, [to be effective] 'justice must satisfy the appearance of justice.'"[19] How would the Court—and Rehnquist—deal with this issue?

Third, it was highly unusual for the Supreme Court to grant certiorari based on the government defendants' petition. When federal appeals courts reverse trial court dismissals based on FRCP 12(b)(6), they almost always send the case directly back to the trial court for reconsideration, applying any special instructions the court of appeals left in its decision. This is so for two very basic reasons. First, courts prefer to be as economical and efficient as possible when it comes to moving litigation through their dockets. When courts of appeals reverse lower court dismissals for failure to properly state a cause of action, it in no way guarantees a victory for the plaintiffs at trial. Rule 12(b)(6) motions are made pretrial—there has been no discovery, no trial testimony, and no consideration of this evidence by a judge or jury at that point in litigation proceedings. Second, even if the plaintiffs were to win their case at trial, the issue would still be reviewable by courts of appeals. For the Supreme Court to agree to hear this case at this stage in the litigation was a breach of the established model of judicial economy.

Finally, there was the question whether Article III standing doctrine in cases like *Tatum* created an insurmountable paradox for potential plaintiffs by holding, in effect, that plaintiffs could show injury if they were "immobilized by fear," but if they really were immobilized by fear, they would not be willing to come to court to allege this injury. For political activists, this presented a very real problem. If leaders of such organizations appeared before courts on behalf of their membership to assert a First Amendment chill by government activity, the government defendants could counter that argument by pointing out the fact that by appearing before federal courts—representing a branch of the U.S. government—plaintiffs apparently did not feel so cowed by their government that they feared to exercise their First Amendment rights before such bodies, and therefore could not meet the actual injury-in-fact standard set forth under Article III standing doctrine.

These issues would provide dramatic subtext to the *Tatum* parties as they prepared their arguments to make before the Supreme Court. But the real question facing the Court, the *Tatum* parties, and future plaintiffs seeking to challenge secret government surveillance programs required the justices to reevaluate the judicial doctrine of standing as it applied to the more modern concept of the chilling effects of the state's gaze. In order to understand this sometimes elusive doctrine, we need to examine its history.

4

The Doctrine of Article III Standing

The Supreme Court has described the judicial doctrine of standing as a "bedrock requirement" for federal court jurisdiction under Article III's case-or-controversy prerequisite.[1] A superficial reading of the current understanding of the doctrine is fairly straightforward. In short, standing is granted only to plaintiffs who can show a particularized "injury in fact" that is caused by the defendant(s) and that is likely to be redressable by the court. One need not look much further into the many cases where the question of standing has been at issue to realize that the application of this doctrine can vary quite wildly, and often raises heated discussions between judges on the proper interpretation of these principles. The exact boundaries of this doctrine have been so elusive, in fact, that scholars have referred to it as the "Rorschach test of federal courts."[2] But how can a practice so critical to the ability (or inability) of plaintiffs to bring their grievances before a court in the hope of obtaining relief be so hard for judges to pin down? Does this lack of a common understanding unjustly keep some plaintiffs from getting through the courthouse doors? And if this is the case, why do we tolerate such a requirement in the first place? What was the intended purpose of this "bedrock requirement," and if judges have difficulty with the concept, how are non-lawyer plaintiffs supposed to grapple with it?

Even attempts to get at standing's core principles by seeking out the origins of the doctrine can be frustrating. Again, the glib response to this question would point the reader back in the direction of Article III's case-or-controversy requirement, with possible detours through the courts' historical focus on private rights, or the very real concerns of judicial economy and docket management. Exploring further down this rabbit hole, one will find that some scholars have—quite persuasively—suggested that our current concept of standing doctrine is an invention of progressive judges during the New Deal era intending to protect the nascent concept of the federal administrative state from judicial review.[3]

Still others have claimed that, whatever the rules of standing doctrine once were, they were manipulated beyond recognition by the Burger and Rehnquist Courts in an attempt to reverse expansion of federal power and liberal doctrines such as civil rights and environmentalism.[4] There are important truths to be found in each of these explanations, of course, and the purpose of this chapter is to pull together enough of these threads to—hopefully—weave a rope strong enough to pull us through the Court's reasoning in the *Tatum* case.

In order to keep this chapter on standing doctrine to a manageable length—indeed, entire books are written on this topic alone—we will limit the discussion to the question of standing most relevant to the *Tatum* plaintiffs. That is, how do courts consider the right of plaintiffs to challenge the policies of government agencies or officials in federal courts, and how have those considerations developed over time? Answering this question, as it turns out, is not as straightforward a task as common sense might indicate. Courts' readings of the Article III standing requirement have been remarkably inconsistent over the history of U.S. jurisprudence. This judicial inconsistency has been no small source of frustration to scholars trying to articulate a generalized theory, to judges trying to apply the interpretation of other courts as precedent, and to plaintiffs trying to convince courts to hear their grievances. For the purposes of this chapter, we will adopt an instrumentalist view in an attempt to understand and explain standing doctrine through the lens of the functions courts have strived to satisfy.

U.S. courts have relied on the constitutional separation of powers requirement as the foundation upon which standing doctrine rests. Professor Joseph Vining, in his book *Legal Identity*, used a number of methods in an attempt to deconstruct the reasoning behind the evolution of standing doctrine.[5] In a particularly imaginative section on private standing to challenge public laws, Vining imagines a scenario in which an individual arrives at a courthouse with a complaint about a government decision. When asked by a court clerk whether she was harmed by this decision, the potential plaintiff is somewhat confused by the question, saying, "I am affected by it, in a way I do not like. I hurt, and since I say the decision is illegal, I should think society would not like its effect on me either. Is that harm? How do you define *harm*?" This imaginary exchange gets right to the heart of a common disconnect in legal interpretation: What does the law mean by words like "harm" or "injury"? Is it a dictionary definition or something else? Is it a static understanding of the term or can it change over time? After a lengthy dialogue on the definition, the clerk asks the question in a different way: "We asked whether you were *harmed*. Can you tell us whether this decision harmed *you*?" This question only confuses Vining's fictional plaintiff further, so the clerk explains that "the question is whether there is an effect upon you that sets you apart from everyone else," because if the court cannot set this plaintiff apart in such a way, "we can't see *you*. We see everyone instead."

This question directly reflects the role that U.S. federal courts have evolved for themselves, as arbiters of disputes between individuals and not disputes between large segments of society. These larger disputes, courts have reasoned, are political questions best left to the legislature and the voters. In fact, courts have said, this limitation upon judicial power has been directly imposed by the Constitution itself through its central philosophy of separation of powers. If you were to look for this explicit limitation in the text of the document itself, however, you might come away disappointed, since the principle of separation of powers is not articulated in the words themselves, but rather in the structure of the Constitution. By separately defining the legislative, executive, and judicial powers of the federal government (Articles I, II, and III, respectively), the Constitution laid out a model where each branch of government was restricted to its own sphere and was forbidden from expanding into another branch's legal territory. If courts, therefore, elected to decide cases that would otherwise fall within the purview of either the executive or legislative branch, they would violate the constitutional separation of powers principle. The Supreme Court firmly adopted this philosophy in the 1984 case of *Allen v. Wright*.[6]

In *Allen*, parents of black children attending public schools in districts undergoing desegregation sought to challenge the rules and guidelines implemented by the Internal Revenue Service (IRS) to deny tax-exempt status to racially discriminatory private schools. The plaintiffs' complaint did not appear to be controversial, since, just a year earlier, the Supreme Court had held that racially discriminatory private schools could not qualify for tax-exempt status.[7] The *Allen* plaintiffs were simply asking the Court to fulfill its part of the bargain by adopting standards and guidelines that would effectively carry out the Court's ruling. More specifically, plaintiffs argued that the ongoing process of desegregation in their districts was being hampered by the existence of racially discriminatory private schools, many of which were founded as a direct response to desegregation policies. These impediments were enabled by IRS standards that continued to reward and encourage discriminatory private schools, which limited the plaintiffs' ability to enjoy equal access to education. The plaintiffs were denied the opportunity to argue the merits of their case, however, as the Court dismissed their case for lack of Article III standing.

In her majority opinion, Justice Sandra Day O'Connor wrote that, while the plaintiffs met the standing requirement of personal injury through their claims of denied access to equal educational opportunities, they did not show that this harm could be "fairly traceable" to the policies of the IRS, and therefore did not meet the requirements for standing in a federal court. O'Connor cited the separation of powers principle as the "single basic idea" behind standing doctrine, noting that this idea does not just mean that plaintiffs lacking standing have complaints that are merely outside the judicial sphere. Instead, she went much farther by stating that the separation of powers principle is the basis upon which the standing requirement must be interpreted. This may seem like a distinction without a difference, but it was a considerable expansion of judicial discretion to dismiss due to lack of standing.

The plaintiffs in *Allen* were held to have shown no fairly traceable injury partly because the Court's recognition of their harm would "have the federal courts as virtually continuing monitors of the wisdom and soundness of Executive action," thus infringing upon the executive branch's constitutional sphere. This reasoning went beyond the consideration of separation of powers as a mere justiciability question, but was instead to be interwoven into standing itself by keeping federal courts out of the business of the other branches of government, which in turn "counsels against recognizing standing in a case brought . . . to seek a restructuring of the apparatus established by the Executive Branch to fulfill its legal duties." O'Connor's separation of powers–based reasoning serves to filter out a case if the plaintiff's allegations or interest took the court to places beyond the judiciary's proper constitutional role.

But this assessment raises yet another problem: Who defines the official boundaries of the separation of powers principle? Many of the cases that reach the Supreme Court get to that stage based upon questions that inherently contain principled disagreements over the proper roles of our branches of government, so it is not as if there exists a single definition of separation of powers doctrine. Using our instrumentalist lens, we can gaze across the expanse of cases that attempt to wrestle with this difficult question, to find multiple such definitions based on their functional goals: to ensure that the right parties are heard (the most obvious goal of the "cases and controversies" requirement under Article III), to avoid political questions, and to prevent the improper use of the courts by the other branches of government as a tool to fight their internecine battles.

The most intuitive reason that standing doctrine exists at all can be directly gleaned from the Constitution's requirements for the judiciary as laid out in Article III. The Supreme Court has pointed out, however, that this "cases" or "controversies" requirement has "an iceberg quality, containing beneath their surface simplicity submerged complexities which go to the very heart of our constitutional form of government."[8] As a sort of baseline, the Court has interpreted this complexity to mean that Article III limits "the business of federal courts to questions presented in an adversary context and in a form historically viewed as capable of resolution through the judicial process."[9] Anything beyond this scope is outside the constitutional power of the courts, and falls into the realm of one of the other branches of government. The most straightforward litmus test courts have at their disposal, therefore, is to restrict entry only to those plaintiffs whose complaints appear to satisfy this prerequisite.

But this seems too easy. Do plaintiffs actually show up in federal courts without an actual stake in their case, or for that matter, without a case at all? The answer, of course, is yes in both cases. A well-known example of this can be found in the 1911 case of *Muskrat v. United States*, where plaintiffs asked the Court to determine the constitutional validity of an act of Congress to increase the number of people entitled to participate in the distribution of Cherokee lands and funds.[10] The plaintiffs alleged that they had an interest in the property at stake, and they sought to have the legislation in question declared to be unconstitutional and void by the Court. The plaintiffs argued that their basis for challenging this act came from yet another act of Congress that purported to grant the Court jurisdiction over their cases, going so far as to list them by name in the text. Despite what appeared to be express congressional approval to hear the plaintiffs' case, the Supreme Court refused to grant standing, however, since it was constitutionally forbidden from giving a "judicial determination, final in this court, of the constitutional validity of an act of Congress." What the *Muskrat* plaintiffs' case lacked was an actual case or controversy, and the other branches of government did not have the constitutional power to extend the Court's duties to areas that were not "properly judicial." Because the *Muskrat* plaintiffs did not have a real stake in the outcome of the case, there was no standing.

Given this requirement, plaintiffs might be therefore tempted to manufacture a controversy that might get them through the courthouse door. Such "collusive actions" also fail to meet the standing requirement, however. In 1943, for example, a tenant of a residential property named Edward Roach brought a lawsuit in the Northern District of Indiana against his landlord, Dick Johnson, alleging that the building he lived in was within a "defense rental area" as defined by the Emergency Price Control Act of 1942, and he had therefore been charged more in rent than the maximum amount allowed under the regulation.[11] The district court dismissed the complaint, finding that the act was unconstitutional. The U.S. government then intervened, and moved to reopen the case to challenge the assertion that it did not involve a real case or controversy. As the Supreme Court heard, the original plaintiff, Roach, brought his complaint under a false name, and did so as a "friendly suit" at defendant Johnson's request, had never met with the attorney of record, had not even read the complaint, and only discovered his involvement in the case when he read about it in the local newspaper. The Court vacated the judgment of the lower court, holding that there was no jurisdiction in this case, where "[e]ven in a litigation where only private rights are involved, the judgment will not be allowed to stand where one of the parties has dominated the conduct of the suit by payment of the fees of both."

This requirement of actual legal adversity between the parties is not a mere whim of federal courts; it functions to better illuminate the finer points of the issues at stake in the case. In the 1962 case of *Baker v. Carr*, the Supreme Court was asked to consider a complaint brought by Tennessee voters who sought a declaration that a state apportionment statute was an unconstitutional deprivation of equal protection under the Fourteenth Amendment.[12] The state statute in question was a 1901 Tennessee law that apportioned the members of its legislative body, the General Assembly, among the state's counties. The formula the state used to allocate legislative representation was based on the total number of qualified voters resident in the respective counties. The 1901 law dropped the requirement that the state conduct its own census, and opted to use the federal census as a basis for apportionment. Over the six decades between 1901 and 1961, the population of Tennessee grew considerably, from 2,020,616 (with 487,380 eligible voters) to 3,567,089 (with 2,092,891 eligible voters), and the relative sizes of the counties changed as well. The *Baker* plaintiffs argued that the 1901 apportionment statute was therefore "unconstitutional and obsolete." The plaintiffs also pointed out that changing this law was further made impossible by the unfair apportionment, since the counties who were happy with the status quo were given more representative clout in the state legislature.

The district court dismissed the *Baker* plaintiffs' case for lack of subject matter jurisdiction and further holding that no claim had been stated upon which relief could be granted. The Supreme Court disagreed. Justice William J. Brennan, writing for the majority, stated that because "the very nature of the controversy was Federal, . . . jurisdiction existed," and "the subject matter is within the federal judicial power defined in Art. III, s 2." In *Baker*, "the appellants [had] alleged such a personal stake in the outcome of the controversy as to assure that concrete adverseness which sharpens the presentation of issues" because they sought "relief in order to protect or vindicate an interest of their own" by "asserting a plain, direct and adequate interest in maintaining the effectiveness of their votes." Thus, truly adverse parties make for sharper issues, and sharper issues give courts a better handle on whether or not the case before them is constitutionally appropriate for them to hear, and does not incur the risk of treading on the toes of the other branches of government. Or as the Supreme Court put it, this function of standing doctrine "tends to assure that the legal questions presented to the court will be resolved, not in the rarified atmosphere of a debating society, but in a concrete factual context conducive to a realistic appreciation of the consequences of judicial action."[13]

A related, but less obvious, function of standing is to ensure the proper role of the judiciary in a democracy. This function goes beyond the constitutional requirements of court jurisdiction, and looks to the "proper—and properly limited—role of the courts" in our society generally.[14] This is a somewhat more philosophical take on separation of powers, and this functional aspect of standing has been the source of a fair amount of criticism that points out that courts often use this reasoning to avoid cases they just do not want to hear. Scholars and commentators have repeatedly pointed out how this functional aspect of standing doctrine has been used by courts to construct artificial obstacles to bar plaintiffs from making their case that government actors are failing to meet constitutional standards.

In *Allen v. Wright*, for example, the Supreme Court denied standing to plaintiffs who wished to challenge the constitutionality of IRS rules and procedures that appeared to encourage and reward racially discriminatory private schools by granting them tax-exempt status. As discussed above, the Court's reasoning in *Allen* went far afield of the previous few decades of decisions on standing to focus on the doctrine's interpretation through the separation of powers lens. While it might be a somewhat straightforward task to draw a line between the explicit language in Article III and the implicit structural facets of the Constitution to reach a doctrine that considers separation of powers principles in standing analysis, it becomes a hazier and more cumbersome prospect to focus on the "pervasive and fundamental notion of separation of powers" as "the single basic idea" behind standing.[15]

In *Allen*, Justice O'Connor applied this newly developed principle to reject standing for the plaintiffs, reasoning that the "line of causation" between the IRS policies and the injuries to the plaintiffs was "attenuated at best," and that it was "pure speculation" for anyone to assume that a change in IRS guidelines would change the private schools' racially discriminatory behavior. This reasoning by the Court was explicitly based on an expanded view of separation of powers–based standing that thus forbade federal courts from becoming "virtually continuing monitors of the wisdom and soundness of Executive action." In other words, according to the Court's decision in *Allen*, plaintiffs who asked federal courts to evaluate the legal and constitutional actions of the other branches of governments were now subject to a much higher degree of scrutiny as a threshold matter. But this reasoning, while perhaps more difficult to pin down at the margins, does have a basis in separation of powers principles. When plaintiffs bring complaints of injuries before federal courts that are shared with so many other citizens that they become "generalized grievances" in the eyes of the judiciary, courts suggest that a democratic society is best equipped to deal with these issues through the political process, and not through the courts. But a paradox emerges from this line of thinking. If these sorts of "generalized grievances" are denied standing due to the sheer number of those harmed, how does that square with the long-standing harm test that merely requires a plaintiff to allege an injury in fact, and does not incorporate into its analysis the possible fact that others may also share the same injury?

This conundrum around standing became especially apparent in a series of environmental cases that private citizens' groups brought before federal courts in the 1990s. The roots of these cases can be traced to the introduction of wide-ranging environmental legislation during the early 1970s. When Congress amended the Clean Air Act (CAA) in 1970, it took a page from its recent innovations in civil rights legislation and gave citizens the right to bring suit both against the administrator of the Environmental Protection Agency (EPA) for failing to enforce its own standards, and against the polluters themselves for failure to adhere to the statute.[16] Similarly, when President Nixon signed into law the Clean Water Act (CWA) in 1972, it included similar "citizen suit" provisions in its language.[17] Subsequent environmental laws included their own versions of this language to enable actions brought by private citizens, rather than government attorneys general. This relatively novel ability for private citizens to enforce federal laws soon began to have a significant impact on environmental policy, with the EPA amending or adding to its own rules in order to satisfy plaintiff complaints.[18] As we have seen in this chapter, however, these citizen suits would not be possible if the plaintiffs in those cases were not granted standing by federal courts. Could Congress thus give potential plaintiffs a boost over the standing bar with these citizen suit provisions?

This was the primary question the Supreme Court considered in 1987, when a number of environmental groups brought a citizen suit against a holder of a pollutant discharge permit, claiming that the defendant had exceeded the discharge limitations given in that permit.[19]

The plaintiffs claimed that between 1981 and 1984, the defendants had repeatedly violated the conditions of their discharge permit, and had recorded these violations in discharge monitoring reports collected during this time. In 1984 the plaintiffs brought a citizen suit in the Eastern District of Virginia, which granted summary judgment to the plaintiffs. The defendant appealed this decision in 1985, arguing that federal courts had no jurisdiction under the CWA, since it allowed citizen suits only against those who were "alleged to be in violation" of the act, noting the present tense of the clause. Since the defendant was no longer in violation of the discharge permit, the plaintiffs could not have standing in this case. The question the Court considered was whether the CWA "confers federal jurisdiction over citizen suits for wholly past violations," ultimately finding that it did not, and reversed the lower court's decision. The *Gwaltney* Court, in an opinion that contained more than a few instances of the sarcastic wit for which Justice Antonin Scalia would become well-known, acknowledged the ambiguity of the clause's language in the otherwise "limpid prose" of Congress, and interpreted that ambiguity against plaintiffs' standing under the act. In his concurring opinion, Scalia asserted that standing was the chief issue in this case, arguing that "under sound practice" courts should "require" "such consideration of standing."

To students of Scalia's judicial philosophy, this approach to standing would come as no surprise. In 1983, while a judge on the U.S. Court of Appeals for the D.C. Circuit, Scalia published a provocative essay on the doctrine of standing that clarified this judicial reasoning as a necessary component of the constitutional principle of separation of powers.[20] His principal argument rested on his distinction between two different kinds of cases: "[W]hen an individual who is the very *object* of a law's requirement or prohibition seeks to challenge it, he always has standing." Otherwise, standing should be generally withheld from "the plaintiff [who] is complaining of an agency's unlawful *failure* to impose a requirement or prohibition upon *someone else*." The second scenario asks the judiciary to enter territory that belongs to another branch of government, specifically, the executive. Further, Scalia argued that Article III limits "even the power of Congress to convert generalized benefits into legal rights." The doctrine of standing is, in Scalia's view, "an essential means of restricting the courts to their assigned role of protecting minority

rather than majority interests," which were better addressed in the political realm in a democratic society. Courts should not become "a group
that is supposed to decide what is good for the people."

In 1990 Justice Scalia continued to develop this new theory of standing as a measure of the judiciary's proper role in a democratic society,
when members of the National Wildlife Federation (NWF), a private
environmental education and advocacy organization, brought a citizen
suit under the Administrative Procedure Act (APA), challenging the reclassification of 1,250 tracts of federally held land, which opened them
up for mining and mineral exploration.[21] Under the APA, "[a] person
suffering legal wrong . . . or adversely affected or aggrieved by agency
action" could seek judicial review in such cases.[22] The Supreme Court
granted certiorari in this case on the question of whether the plaintiffs'
members were injured by the agency's action, analyzing this issue si-
multaneously under the separate lenses of constitutional standing and
statutory interpretation. Writing for the majority, Scalia collapsed these
two modes into one issue of standing. He pointed to the affidavits submitted by two members of the plaintiff organization claiming personal
injury due to the reclassification of the land parcels in question. These
affidavits claimed that they used the recreational lands near the tracts
in question, but not the actual tracts themselves. They did not offer any
proof that this recreational use of adjacent land would be harmed by
possible mineral exploration or mining, nor did they offer any sort of
personal connection to the reclassified tracts in question. While this
was enough to satisfy the lower court of appeals that the plaintiffs had
standing to bring their case, it was not enough for Scalia. The dissenting
opinion, written by Justice Harry Blackmun, looked to the record from
the lower court and pointed out how the plaintiffs had offered "ample
support" for their "contention that mining activities can be expected to
cause severe environmental damage" to the recreational lands adjacent
to the reclassified tracts. But this was the minority view. In a 5–4 decision, the Court elected to once again raise the bar for Article III standing
using its functional definition of the judiciary's proper role, stating that
"[e]xcept where Congress explicitly provides for our correction of the
administrative process at a higher level of generality, we intervene in the
administration of the laws only when, and to the extent that, a specific
'final agency action' has an actual or immediately threatened effect."

Two years later, Scalia was offered yet another opportunity to further elevate the bar of standing doctrine (as well as further establish this view of standing in contemporary jurisprudence). The case of *Lujan v. Defenders of Wildlife* was a challenge to a rule promulgated by the secretary of the interior interpreting a section of the Endangered Species Act (ESA).[23] The complaint was brought by a conservation group under the ESA's citizen suit provision, which provides that "any person may commence a civil suit on his own behalf (A) to enjoin any person, including the United States and any other governmental instrumentality or agency . . . who is alleged to be in violation of any provision in this chapter."[24] The complaint alleged that a 1983 regulation by the Fish and Wildlife Service and the National Marine Fisheries Service, which overruled its 1978 version and interpreted the ESA to apply only to actions taken within the United States, was in error, and sought a declaratory judgment of this by the courts. Their injury, said the plaintiffs, came from the lack of consultation with the agencies with respect to "certain funded activities abroad" that "increase the rate of extinction of endangered and threatened species," which cause harm by preventing the plaintiffs from observing these animals. The two affidavits offered by the plaintiffs in support of their case stated that the members had visited the areas of these animals' habitats in the past, and would be injured if these animals were no longer around when they visited these sites "in the future."

The lower court of appeals in this case held that the plaintiffs had standing on two bases. First, the court of appeals found the plaintiffs' affidavits sufficient to show both interest and injury to satisfy the Article III standing requirement. Second, they observed that the plaintiffs had suffered a "procedural injury" stemming from the citizen suit provision of the ESA. The appeals court held that, under the act, anyone can file suit in federal court to challenge any agency's failure to follow rulemaking procedure, even if they could not allege any other discrete injury that resulted from that procedural failure. Scalia rejected both of these arguments, using language that would come to represent the state of the art in standing doctrine for decades to come.

Scalia began by setting the stage with respect to the Court's current thinking around standing doctrine. This jurisprudence, he argued, could be boiled down to an "irreducible constitutional minimum" of three elements. First, the plaintiff must have suffered an "injury in fact," which is both "concrete and particularized" and "actual or imminent, not 'conjectural' or 'hypothetical.'" Second, there must be a causal connection between the injury and the action, such that the injury is "fairly traceable to the challenged action of the defendant, and not the result of the independent action of some third party not before the court." Finally, it must be "likely" and not merely "speculative" that the injury will be "redressed by a favorable decision." Using this "constitutional minimum," Scalia held that the plaintiffs failed to meet their burden under this test, failing to show both injury and redressability.

With the first basis of the court of appeals' reasoning to grant standing thus disposed of, Scalia moved on to the idea of "procedural injury," which appeared to be especially rankling to him as seen through the functional lens of the proper role of the judiciary in society. He found this complaint smacking of "impermissible generalized grievance" that "does not state an Article III case or controversy" without "draining those requirements of meaning," citing cases in the past few years where the Court had denied standing to "a taxpayer suit challenging the Government's failure to disclose the expenditures of the Central Intelligence Agency," "a citizen-taxpayer suit" contending that it was illegal for "Members of Congress to hold commissions in the military Reserves," and "a citizen suit to prevent a condemned criminal's execution," all of which were categorized as generalized grievances. Even though, as Scalia admits, these cases typically involve violations of constitutional procedures and principles by government agencies, "there is absolutely no basis for making the Article III inquiry turn on the source of the asserted right." To do otherwise—even at the behest of Congress—would be to discard the principles behind standing doctrine that restrict the courts to their own business as functionally defined by a democratic society.

Scalia's opinion in *Lujan* would prove to be one of the most important cases on the issue of standing, not only for its impact on the judiciary's understanding of the doctrine, but also for the rather large number of federal statutes it plowed through to get there, invalidating or calling into question the environmental and regulatory citizen suit. *Lujan* stood for the proposition that a plaintiff's alleged "injury in fact" (as understood pre-*Lujan*) was neither necessary nor sufficient to establish standing; instead, the main question was whether the law gave plaintiffs a cognizable cause of action, by statute, common law, or the Constitu-tion. The post-*Lujan* "injury in fact" test placed a high degree of impor-tance on the injury being both imminent and non-speculative. Under this new test, someone with a complaint about government actions—or inactions—whose only interest was in the proper enforcement of the law or general adherence to constitutional principles was now less likely to attain standing. The reason for this outcome can seem somewhat silly to the uninitiated, since it seemed to require the plaintiff to show an injury to her property, even if that fact hung on trivialities.

As discussed earlier in the chapter, Joseph Vining explained the basis for this philosophy in *Legal Identity* during his imaginary conversation between a potential plaintiff and a court clerk. In the conversation, the clerk patiently explains that the injuries that can require a court to act can be summarized under the headings of *liberty* and *property*, because this follows the constitutionally limited role the judiciary has "to pre-serve or allocate the power of individuals in our society." Just as with any other government entity, courts are authorized to act only when they have been legally authorized to do so. The irony of this arrangement is, of course, in the fact that a court's action outside this authorized role in order to address a plaintiff's complaint about a government's unau-thorized actions, would itself be creating yet another unauthorized gov-ernment action, doing very little to reduce the overall level of illegality in society. The court's role in a democratic society is to settle disputes between individuals, not between large populations within a society— these latter disputes are best left to the political or legislative process. Since the courts thus see actors in society not as groups but as individu-als, it presumes that each of these individual citizens is free to choose his or her own actions, and must be responsible for the consequences of those actions. Any of those individual citizens in a case before the court must therefore show which of the categories of injury recognized by the court his or her complaint falls under.

After *Lujan*, these two categories—especially that of property—were brought to the forefront of injury in fact and the standing question. The requirement that a plaintiff's injury be both imminent and non-speculative further elevated the bar of Article III standing. In *Lujan*, for example, since the plaintiffs' affidavits only alleged the facts that they had visited the habitats of the endangered animals in the past, and indicated an intent to visit those sites again sometime in the future, the Court would not grant standing, since the "[p]ast exposure to illegal conduct does not in itself show a present case or controversy . . . if unaccompanied by any continuing, present adverse effects." A mere "intent" to return to the endangered animals' habitats "some day" without "any description of concrete plans, or indeed even any specification of *when* the some day will be—do[es] not support a finding of the 'actual or imminent' injury that our cases require." To put it another way, had the plaintiffs booked a flight to the areas in question, or had even made firm plans to visit those sites, the Court might have granted them standing. How else might this rather formalistic requirement take shape? Could consumers be required to purchase a product known to be dangerous or defective before their claim of harm—likely here a complaint of diminished opportunity—is not too speculative? If a packaged food company is adding known carcinogens to its products, would consumers first have to buy (and consume) these carcinogenic products before they would have standing to challenge government regulation of that product?

The difficulty in answering these questions is nothing new to the judiciary's ongoing struggle to clarify standing doctrine, as we have seen. In the 2000 case of *Friends of the Earth, Inc. v. Laidlaw Environmental Services, Inc.*, for example, the Supreme Court heard arguments regarding an environmental group's complaints about the effect the defendant's pollutant discharge—which exceeded the limits set by its permits—was having on land that the plaintiff's members once used to "fish, camp, swim, and picnic in and near" as teenagers, and would like to do so once again, but could not due to the harmful pollution. These facts were quite similar to those of *Lujan*, in that plaintiffs only alleged a past use of the land along with an unspecific plan to use the land in a similar fashion sometime in the future. Yet despite these strong similarities, the Court ruled in favor of the plaintiff, holding that it had Article III standing to bring a citizen suit. What led the Court to this conclusion regarding standing in a case so similar to *Lujan* that, at first blush, should have been thrown out based on that case's precedent?

Justice Ruth Bader Ginsburg's majority opinion cited the imminent harm/injury in fact requirement of *Lujan*, and reiterated the Article III requirement that a plaintiff show "injury in fact" that is "concrete and particularized," "actual or imminent," "fairly traceable to the defendant's actions," and "redressable by a favorable decision." In *Lujan*, the Court held that the plaintiff could not be granted standing based on mere "general averments" and "conclusory allegations," but the majority saw nothing improbable about the plaintiff's fears resulting from the defendant's conduct in this case. The possibility of "economic and aesthetic harms" was a reasonable basis for the Court's majority to find injury in fact and grant standing to the plaintiff. Predictably, Justice Scalia, the author of the *Lujan* opinion, disagreed with the majority. He pointed out that the plaintiff's affidavits in this case were just as vague as those offered by the plaintiffs in *Lujan*, and by granting the plaintiff standing in this case, the Court was "marry[ing] private wrong with public remedy," which violated that functional role of the judiciary in a democratic society.

Given these quite different readings by members of the same Supreme Court, one could be forgiven for being confused about the exact dimensions of Article III standing doctrine. As these examples show, the parsing of details by courts to decide just who can and cannot show "injury in fact" sufficient to be granted standing can prove profoundly unsatisfying, even to lawyers and judges. Courts will hear some cases that appear to have nearly identical facts as cases that have been rejected by other courts. Judges can write opinions regarding standing based on distinctions so fine that most of us (again, even lawyers and judges) would find ridiculous. This confusion is not arbitrary, of course. The legal interpretation of constitutional language is difficult and can pose intractable rhetorical problems that courts are forced to resolve. The functional approach to this problem provides some additional clarity, but it is far from a foolproof guide to standing doctrine. And even when a court's reasoning when deciding standing is made clearer through the functional lens, the patterns that emerge can be disquieting, and hint at politically based reasoning by what is supposed to be an impartial court.

The careful reader will also note at this point that much of standing doctrine was formulated within the last century or so, and a significant proportion of this jurisprudence was decided in the last few decades. In fact, the history of formal standing doctrine is quite recent. The first actual reference to "standing" by a court was not until 1944, and throughout the history of the Supreme Court, the term has been discussed as an explicit doctrine unto itself only 222 times. Of those 222 cases, 7 were decided between 1928 and 1945, 20 were decided between

1946 and 1972, and the remaining 195 were decided since 1973. The use of "injury in fact" as a prerequisite for standing first appeared in 1970, and then became part of the formal test for standing only in the environmental cases of the 1990s. The doctrine is, therefore, a relatively young one, although it could well be argued that it has been in slow gestation since the late eighteenth century. The shift from the general idea of a "legal wrong" to one of "legal injury" began to take shape in the early 1970s, with the emergence of a new test—an early version of the "injury in fact" test—that would finally be supplanted by our modern concept of standing doctrine stemming from *Lujan* and following cases, starting in the 1990s.

Which brings us back to the case of *Laird v. Tatum*, whose arguments were heard by the Supreme Court on March 27, 1972, over twenty years prior to the Court's decision in *Lujan*. What was the state of standing doctrine when the nine justices gathered to hear this case? More specifically, what were the Supreme Court's views regarding a plaintiff's ability to challenge government programs, laws, or regulations on constitutional grounds? Even more specifically, how did the Court feel about cases brought based only on the deterring or "chilling" effect of government actions on a plaintiff's First Amendment rights? Indeed, Article III standing doctrine was not the only factor providing context to *Laird*. Other legal, political, and social forces had been simmering throughout post–World War II America, and the heat had been steadily increasing during this period. The political turbulence of the 1960s and the subsequent focus on constitutional civil rights provided an appropriate environment for this new cause of action to take shape in U.S. courts, with the First Amendment to the Constitution becoming a focal point for legal challenges to controversial government activities.

In 1962 L. B. Sullivan, a Montgomery, Alabama, city commissioner, sued the *New York Times* for libel in an Alabama state court. Sullivan's claim was based on the *Times'* reporting of civil rights demonstrations in Alabama from 1956 through 1960. During this time, the *Times* published an advertisement in support of the nascent civil rights movement that made claims that students had been abused by Alabama police officers following a peaceful protest in Montgomery. Sullivan asserted that this advertisement libeled him, since his duties included the supervision of the police department in question, and brought suit. The case eventually made its way up to the Alabama Supreme Court, which affirmed judgment in favor of Sullivan and awarded him $500,000. The case was appealed to the U.S. Supreme Court, which heard arguments on January 6, 1964.[25] On March 9, the Court overturned the Alabama Supreme Court's decision, holding that the law applied by the Alabama courts infringed upon the constitutional protections for freedom of speech and freedom of the press, and that, in order for a libel action brought by a public official to succeed, the official must first prove that the statements in question were made with actual malice. This term was defined by the court as knowledge by the defendant that the defamatory statement was false, or was made with reckless disregard as to its truthfulness. In his concurring opinion, Justice Hugo Black noted approvingly that the Court had demonstrated the "chilling effect of the Alabama libel laws on First Amendment freedoms," and that the country should not be willing to take the risk that "men who injure and oppress the people under their administration [and] provoke them to cry out and complain" will also be empowered to "make that very complaint the foundation of new oppressions and prosecutions."

In a 1965 case that hewed somewhat closer to the fact pattern later seen in *Tatum*, the plaintiffs were a civil rights organization and associated activists working in Louisiana. In *Dombrowski v. Pfister*, the plaintiffs sought to enjoin the defendants from prosecuting or threatening to prosecute them for alleged violations of the Louisiana Subversive Activities and Communist Control Law and the Louisiana Communist Propaganda Control Law.[26] When the plaintiffs brought their case before the U.S. District Court for the Eastern District of Louisiana, that court dismissed their complaint for failure to state a claim upon which relief could be granted. On appeal, the Supreme Court reversed the lower court, holding that not only was the plaintiffs' complaint sufficient for standing, but also that the applicable Louisiana laws were unconstitutionally vague. Writing for the majority, Justice William J. Brennan noted that the Court pays special attention to statutes that have an "overbroad sweep" or risk the loss or substantial impairment of "those precious rights" articulated in the Constitution. The Court was consistent in its precedent allowing attacks on these overly broad statutes "with no requirement that the person making the attack demonstrate that his own conduct could not be regulated by a statute drawn with the requisite narrow specificity." Brennan explained that the Court "fashioned this exception to the usual rules governing standing" because of the "danger of tolerating, in the area of First Amendment freedoms, the existence of a penal statute susceptible of sweeping and improper application." Since the plaintiffs were able to show proof of the chilling effect on their free expression the prosecutions—and threatened prosecutions—had on their constitutionally protected activity, the Court granted standing and found in favor of the plaintiffs.

The D.C. Court of Appeals had followed this reasoning in *Tatum*. When considering whether the mere chilling effect on First Amendment rights could show injury sufficient to grant standing, the court stated that in suits alleging a First Amendment chill, "immediate and real injury is done to the plaintiff's interest if he *does not speak* or act as he says he wants to." In other words, the injury arose not from an action, but from the plaintiffs' inability to take that action if they so chose. According to the appeals court, the government activity alleged by the *Tatum* plaintiffs was more than an "incidental" burden to constitutionally protected rights, and thus satisfied the Court's requirement of factoring the "severity and scope" of the alleged chilling effects. The jurisprudential pendulum with respect to standing doctrine thus appeared to be swinging the *Tatum* plaintiffs' way in 1972. It remained to be seen, however, whether the Supreme Court—to which a conservative young Department of Justice attorney named William Rehnquist had just been appointed as an associate justice—would agree with that assessment.

5

Before the Supreme Court

On January 7, 1972, just ten weeks prior to the date the Supreme Court was scheduled to hear oral argument in *Laird v. Tatum*, two new associate justices were sworn in to fill the seats vacated by Hugo Black and John Harlan. Both justices had been liberal fixtures on the bench as part of the Court led by Chief Justice Earl Warren, who had retired three years prior, with Warren Burger appointed to the seat on June 23, 1969. With these three appointments, President Nixon was given a rare opportunity to shift the Supreme Court away from the liberal course it had taken under Chief Justice Warren, and steer it toward a more conservative view of the law and a more originalist view of the Constitution. Lewis Powell, a solidly business-oriented corporate lawyer and partner with the prestigious Virginia law firm of Hunton, Williams, Gay, Powell, and Gibson, had been approached by Nixon in 1969 to fill the seat left by Justice Abe Fortas, who had earlier resigned from the Court under a cloud of scandal.[1] Powell, then quite comfortable with his current position as law firm partner and tobacco industry board member, and concerned that his failing eyesight would hinder his abilities to properly serve on the bench, declined the president's offer. When Nixon approached Powell again in 1971, however, this time to fill Justice Hugo Black's seat, Powell finally relented, and accepted the appointment.

Nixon was no friend of the Warren Court, and had actively campaigned on a platform that opposed its decisions over the years. The greatest amount of support for this platform came from the South, and the Nixon team felt that its next Court appointment must, like Powell, also be a Southerner. Nixon briefly considered Senator Robert Byrd, who had attended law school at night while in the Senate, and had never actually practiced law. While this could be seen as a disqualifying characteristic, Nixon saw it as plus. Here was an outsider (to the law and the Court), who was also a Southerner (if one counts West Virginia as part of the South), a former member of the Ku Klux Klan, and certain to win the approval of his fellow senators. Nixon's staffers eventually convinced him that Byrd was never going to be a viable candidate for the Supreme Court. Running out of time under the president's self-imposed deadline of October 21, and unable to find a suitable candidate for the last open seat, Attorney General John Mitchell asked his assistant attorney general, William Rehnquist, to come to his office. Nixon had grown impatient with the candidate vetting process, and was now willing to make the decision on his own. In that spirit, the decision to nominate Rehnquist to the Court was made only by Nixon and Mitchell, although White House counsel John Dean had been recommending Rehnquist for consideration for some time.

Nixon had met Rehnquist only once before, during a White House meeting on the declassification of records. Rehnquist showed up for the meeting wearing thick black glasses, muttonchop sideburns, Hush Puppies shoes, and a pink shirt that clashed with his rather gaudy tie. After Rehnquist left, Nixon turned to John Ehrlichman and asked, "John, who the hell is that clown?"[2] Ehrlichman, who had been a law school classmate of Rehnquist's, was not a fan of Rehnquist as a Supreme Court candidate, as he saw no political advantage to the Nixon administration in his nomination, observing that Rehnquist was a Protestant white male from Arizona. When later asked by a reporter whether he was on the list of possible Nixon nominees to the Court, Rehnquist replied that he was not, since "I'm not from the South, I'm not a woman, and I'm not mediocre." What Rehnquist did have, however, was an excellent academic record, a Supreme Court clerkship under Justice Robert Jackson, and years of solid, if not spectacular, legal experience.

Prior to his Supreme Court appointment, Rehnquist's tenure as assistant attorney general covered much of the same subject matter as the facts in *Tatum*. In fact, while Rehnquist did not directly participate in the briefing or pleadings on behalf of the U.S. government in the *Tatum* case, he was called upon to serve as a witness for the Department of Justice before Senator Ervin's Subcommittee on Constitutional Rights of the Senate Judiciary Committee regarding the constitutionality of the government surveillance programs being investigated by Ervin's committee. Prior to his testimony before the committee, Rehnquist submitted to Ervin a memorandum of law in which he argued that the government surveillance activities being investigated, including those being challenged by the *Tatum* plaintiffs, were constitutional. Moreover, in his public testimony on the topic, he stated that the "full utilization of advanced data gathering techniques is by no means inconsistent with the preservation of personal privacy."[3] In a 1971 speech given to the National Conference of Law Reviews, Rehnquist reiterated his assertion, stating that

> no legitimate interest of any segment of our population would be served by permitting individuals or groups of individuals to prevent by judicial action, the government's gathering information . . . [since] the First Amendment does not prohibit even foolish or unauthorized information gathering by the government.[4]

With this in mind, Rehnquist told the Ervin Committee that courts "have been reluctant, and properly so, to enter upon the supervision of the executive's information-gathering activities so long as such information is not made the basis of a proceeding against a particular individual or individuals."[5]

Not only had Rehnquist generally asserted the constitutionality of these government surveillance programs, but as assistant attorney general, he had made specific references to the facts and merits in the *Tatum* case. When asked by the Ervin Committee whether he thought that citizens are afraid or suspicious of government surveillance, he dismissed the idea out of hand, but acknowledged that "there have always been people who will come forward and sue the government . . . claiming that others were intimidated, but really admitting that they were not intimidated at all." Pressed by the committee, Rehnquist further disagreed with any court's finding of Article III standing for *Tatum*, stating that

> as in the case of *Tatum v. Laird*, . . . an action will lie by private citizens to enjoin the gathering of information by the executive branch where there has been no threat of compulsory process and no pending action against any of the individuals on the part of the Government.[6]

In his public statements and in his writing, Rehnquist had made it crystal clear that his legal opinion opposed the granting of standing for the *Tatum* plaintiffs (or any other plaintiff bringing a similar complaint before a federal court).

In addition to his testimony on the topic, Assistant Attorney General Rehnquist served as spokesman for both the Department of Justice and the executive branch generally on matters relating to military surveillance. Internally, Rehnquist was also asked to coordinate all of the Justice Department's legislative and litigation efforts having to do with surveillance issues, and all evidence relating to such cases was routed through his office. When the Ervin Committee staff asked the Department of Justice to inspect the documents and other evidence relating to its investigation, it was Rehnquist who approved, arranged, and supervised the inspections, which were closely monitored under a set of rules written by Rehnquist himself. When the committee asked for copies of these materials, it received them under the supervision of Rehnquist.

The *Tatum* plaintiffs were therefore understandably unenthusiastic about the prospect of Rehnquist serving as an associate justice when the Supreme Court heard oral arguments in their case. In fact, the plaintiffs were frankly surprised that Rehnquist would be participating in their case at all, considering his public defense of the government's position prior to his appointment as associate justice. The general supposition up to that point had been that Rehnquist would recuse himself from the *Tatum* proceedings, a presumption that had been so strong that the *Tatum* plaintiffs did not even consider raising the issue of Rehnquist's recusal prior to oral argument. Senator Ervin had also considered whether a statement regarding Rehnquist's participation in his committee hearings would be appropriate, but decided against it since it was obvious to everyone that Rehnquist would not participate in *Tatum*.[7] On the day of oral argument, the *Tatum* plaintiffs were dismayed to hear that Justice Rehnquist would, after all, be participating in *Tatum*, and would be sitting for argument that day. The ACLU considered submitting a motion to the Court challenging Rehnquist's right to sit for this case, but Ervin counseled against it, citing an earlier case where a justice had sat for argument, even asking questions of counsel, but ultimately did not participate in the deliberations of the Court. Given this history, and the well-established Court rules regarding judicial recusal, Ervin could not believe that Rehnquist would act any differently. In fact, reasoned Ervin, it was perfectly natural for Rehnquist to want to hear the arguments on the issues he was so closely involved with while assistant attorney general. But despite the quite reasonable assumptions of Ervin and others that Rehnquist would recuse himself from deliberations, this was not to be the case. In fact, Rehnquist would provide the deciding vote in the Court's decision to rule against granting standing to the *Tatum* plaintiffs.

The U.S. solicitor general, Erwin Griswold, opened the oral arguments by asserting that the *Tatum* plaintiffs were trying to sneakily transform their case into something larger—a debate over the proper role of the military in civilian society. Griswold countered that the military had a general (and lawful) responsibility to help keep order when law enforcement needed assistance, and the facts the *Tatum* plaintiffs had asserted were just a matter of "some people [who were] charged with responsibility in this especially at the local level got a little bit too zealous in their activity."[8] While there was a "controversy," Griswold conceded, it was not a "case or controversy" in the constitutional sense. The controversy the *Tatum* plaintiffs were trying to bring into the courtroom was one to be decided in the political or legislative arena. The plaintiffs' complaint of "chill" alone as injury in fact, argued Griswold, was unheard of within standing doctrine. Griswold offered that the best decision the Court could make would be to allow the civilian army authorities to direct their departments, and to leave the judiciary out of it.

Rutgers Law professor Frank Askin, in his oral argument on behalf of the *Tatum* plaintiffs, countered that Griswold had misrepresented the plaintiffs' allegations and circumstances of the case. The only question before the Court that day was "whether the plaintiffs were entitled to a judicial hearing [and] whether [their] uncontested allegations of unauthorized and unconstitutional conduct by the Army earn them the right to their day in Court." Askin argued that this was a class action on behalf of the many citizens and groups whose political activities had been surveilled by over a thousand army agents around the country, not because they had done anything wrong, but based solely on the "specter of civil disturbance" which the army argued justified its actions.

Askin did not get too far into his argument before Justice Potter Stewart interrupted with questions regarding the constitutional basis of the claims. Stewart asked whether this was "basically a First Amendment complaint," or whether the plaintiffs were also arguing that the Fourth Amendment (or others) was also implied in their case. Askin affirmed that, while other amendments may be implied, they were not "the essential gravamen of the complaint." After some additional back-and-forth between Askin and

Justices Douglas, Marshall, and Powell, Chief Justice Burger went right to the objections raised by Judge Hart during the case's first hearing before the district court, asking Askin to "suppose instead of sending agents, the military for whatever reason relied upon newspaper clipping services . . . and fed them into their data banks, would you feel that that violated some constitutional rights of the persons affected?" Askin replied by pointing out that the situation Burger described would be a completely different case on the merits, and was not the plaintiffs' case before the Court. But, asked Burger, weren't these all public meetings? Askin agreed that some of the meetings were public, but other evidence pointed out more clandestine methods used by army agents. Further, argued Askin, the government was going further than the mere statement that public records might be able to be collected by the military. Rather, it was saying that any sort of activity like this by government agents was not reviewable in the first place, preventing courts from even considering these cases on their merits. Askin followed up by borrowing the chief justice's own words from his dissent in *Bivens v. Six Unknown Named Agents*, a case that created a cause of action against the federal government for constitutional violations.[9] Burger, who argued that the decision was not for the courts but for the legislature, conceded that "without some effective sanction, constitutional protection against unlawful conduct by government officials would constitute little more than rhetoric."

Askin yielded the final ten minutes of his time to Senator Ervin, who was there to discuss the "*ultra vires* nature of the military conduct." Chief Justice Burger split the senator's time into two five-minute pieces to be argued before and after their lunch break. Ervin jumped right to the constitutional and statutory powers granted to the military, including the Posse Comitatus Act, which he quoted:

> Whoever, except in cases and under circumstances expressly authorized by the Constitution or an Act of Congress, willfully uses the Army and it has not been admitted, any part of the Army or the Air Force as a posse comitatus or otherwise to execute the laws shall be fined not more than $10,000.00, imprisoned not more than two years, or both.

This, Ervin argued, forbids the use of the Army for detective work. After the lunch break, Ervin continued by stating that the government's argument on the merits of the case was not relevant to the question presented to the Court—the question of Article III standing. Rehnquist was silent throughout the proceedings.

The Supreme Court's opinion in *Laird v. Tatum* was handed down on June 26, 1972. Writing for the five-justice majority, Burger stated that "it is not the role of the judiciary, absent actual present or immediate threatened injury resulting from unlawful government action," to investigate activities of the executive branch of government. Rather than follow the Court's recent decisions regarding First Amendment chill, Burger argued that standing based merely on this allegation was improper, but stated that

> when presented with claims of judicially cognizable injury resulting from military intrusion into the civilian sector, federal courts are fully empowered to consider claims of those asserting such injury; there is nothing in our Nation's history or in this Court's decided cases, including our holding today, that can properly be seen as giving any indication that actual or threatened injury by reason of unlawful activities of the military would go unnoticed or unremedied.

Despite the fact that the *Tatum* plaintiffs maintained throughout their briefs and oral argument—as did the amici in their supporting briefs to the Court—that evidence of injury due to the unconstitutional actions of the Army could and would be introduced to the trial court, if only they could get beyond the standing issue, Burger's opinion made no mention of this, but only noted the materials provided by the solicitor general regarding military directives, which "indicate that the Army's review of the needs of its domestic intelligence activities has indeed been a continuing one and that those activities have since been significantly reduced." This was not an uncontested fact. Both the *Tatum* plaintiffs and the amici—many of whom had direct knowledge of the actual Army surveillance programs—had repeatedly stated that the military intelligence programs against civilians had not been cut short, but rather were continuing. Further, even if those programs had been closed since the *Tatum* case had been in the federal court system, the Supreme Court had previously held that the "voluntary abandonment of a practice does not relieve a court of adjudicating its legality, particularly where the practice is deeply rooted and long standing. For if the case were dismissed as moot appellants would be "free to return to . . . [their] old ways."[10] As shown in previous chapters, military intelligence agencies had been collecting information on the political activities—protected under the First Amendment—of ordinary Americans since the early part of the twentieth century. Surely, the *Tatum* plaintiffs argued, this would count for something.

A majority of the Supreme Court felt otherwise, and denied standing to the *Tatum* plaintiffs. Perhaps unsurprisingly, given his questions posed to Frank Askin during oral argument, Burger focused on the discussion held during Judge Hart's first hearing, observing the seemingly ordinary activity of collecting public information, and citing the statements made during that hearing by plaintiffs' counsel, that the plaintiffs themselves were not chilled or intimidated by the military activities in question, but rather were there representing those American citizens who *did* fear military surveillance, and would therefore not be willing to come to a federal court to publicly offer their complaint. To the casual observer, it might seem obvious that the plaintiffs were not so frightened by the specter of Big Brother that they could not appear in court, and that the statement by plaintiffs' counsel during the initial hearing before Judge Hart was something of a throwaway line. But Burger built the Court's majority opinion around this statement as a foundation.

Burger acknowledged the fact that the Court had recently held that constitutional violations may arise from the chilling effect of government regulations "that fall short of a direct prohibition against the exercise of First Amendment rights." But, he explained,

> In none of these cases . . . did the chilling effect arise merely from the individual's knowledge that a governmental agency was engaged in certain activities or from the individual's concomitant fear that, armed with the fruits of these activities, the agency might in the future take some *other* and additional action detrimental to that individual.

In other words, Burger needed more than the mere fear of government surveillance to find sufficient injury in fact to satisfy the standing requirement. Burger cited recent First Amendment chill cases where "the complainant was either presently or prospectively subject to . . .

regulations" and the "challenged exercise of governmental power was regulatory, proscriptive, or compulsory in nature." Burger allowed that the Court "fully recognize[d] that governmental action may be subject to constitutional challenge even though it has only an indirect effect" on the plaintiff's First Amendment rights, but gave more weight to the "established principle that to entitle a private individual to invoke the judicial power to determine the validity of executive or legislative action he must show that he has sustained or is immediately in danger of sustaining a direct injury as a result of that action." The functionalist definition of the judiciary's proper place in a democratic society overruled the *Tatum* plaintiffs' ability to challenge the actions of the executive branch in this case. The plaintiffs' "perception of the [surveillance] system as inappropriate to the Army's role" or their beliefs "that it is inherently dangerous for the military to be concerned with activities in the civilian sector" were not adequate to meet the Article III standing requirements.

Justices Douglas, Marshall, Brennan, and Stewart strongly disagreed with Burger's opinion, and in their dissents, found that the majority's convenient interpretation of standing doctrine was "too transparent for serious argument." Douglas and Marshall joined in one dissenting opinion to explain, at some length, just how injurious the fear of military surveillance was to the *Tatum* plaintiffs, as it had also been to the nation's founders. According to Douglas and Marshall, the act of turning the Army loose to surveil civilians "was a gross repudiation of our traditions," even if sanctioned by an act of Congress, as it "would raise serious and profound constitutional questions." Quoting Senator Ervin, the justices wrote that the majority's "claim of an inherent executive branch power of investigation and surveillance on the basis of people's beliefs and attitudes may be more of a threat to our internal security than any enemies beyond our borders." The majority's argument that the plaintiffs would have to await the loss of a job, the loss of reputation, or imprisonment before being able to sue "would in practical effect immunize from judicial scrutiny all surveillance activities, regardless of their misuse and their deterrent effect." Douglas argued that the majority's functionalist approach to the judiciary's role was not the intent of standing doctrine. Rather, "the gist of the standing issue is whether the party seeking relief has alleged such a personal stake in the outcome of the controversy as to assure that concrete adverseness which sharpens the presentation of issues upon which the court so largely depends for illumination of difficult constitutional questions."

Justices Brennan, Stewart, and Marshall penned an additional, shorter dissent as well, which was made up almost entirely of a quote from Judge Wilkey, who wrote the court of appeals decision that had granted the *Tatum* plaintiffs standing. As Wilkey put it, "Because the evil alleged in the Army intelligence system is that of overbreadth, . . . and because there is no indication that a better opportunity will later arise to test the constitutionality of the Army's action," the *Tatum* plaintiffs should, at the very least, have their day in court to argue their case on its merits. As Brennan conceded, the plaintiffs "may or may not be able to prove the case they allege, . . . but they are entitled to try."

Vigorous dissents notwithstanding, the *Tatum* plaintiffs were out of luck. But what made their allegations of First Amendment chill substantively different from the other cases that had so recently been before this Court, and in which the Court had found the necessary components of Article III standing? Part of the problem rested on the disposition of the case as it was appealed from the district court opinion to the court of appeals. Since Judge Hart had dismissed the *Tatum* plaintiffs' case without allowing the additional testimonial evidence the plaintiffs had been prepared to offer, the record as it stood before the Supreme Court was not as complete as it could have been. The lack of this evidence precluded the Court from discussing any actual Army surveillance practices, leading Burger to conclude in his opinion that the plaintiffs could not show any real harm in their case, and were therefore attempting to bring their mere disagreement with executive branch decisions before the Court. This "subjective chill" was not enough for the majority to see any real injury in fact.

In fact, the *Tatum* plaintiffs faced something of a catch-22 in their allegations of chilling effects of government surveillance. Burger's majority opinion acknowledged the recent recognition by the Court of First Amendment chill rising to the level of injury in fact, but felt that the plaintiff's fears must arise from something more than "merely . . . the individual's knowledge" of a government agency's activities. According to Burger, cognizable harm from First Amendment chill must be based on government power that compelled the individual to take some action, or proscribed him or her from taking an action. Since, Burger argued, the *Tatum* plaintiffs were neither "presently or prospectively" subject to this sort of government activity, there was no chilling effect, and therefore, no injury in fact. One need look no further than the plaintiffs' own actions to see this fact: According to their own counsel, the plaintiffs were "not people, obviously, who are cowed and chilled," but were quite willing to appear in federal court to challenge the government and "open themselves up to public investigation and public scrutiny." Clearly, these plaintiffs were not intimidated by their government, argued Burger, and thus lacked a "personal stake in the outcome of the controversy essential to standing." This logic seems to articulate the principle that only those plaintiffs too afraid of their government to appear in open court could convince that court that they deserved Article III standing.

Burger did not begin his opinion with the issue of standing, however. Rather, he spent roughly the first half of his opinion establishing the boundaries of the military's legal right—and duty—to establish and maintain an accurate domestic intelligence picture so that, in the event of riots or other civil disorders, the Army could step in to assist civilian police departments to restore order. Citing a federal statute titled Federal Aid for State Governments, Burger pointed out that the president is authorized "to make use of the armed forces to quell insurrection and other domestic violence."[11] In order to properly plan for such a contingency, the military must collect intelligence—as it apparently had been doing in this case—to "be able to respond effectively with a minimum of force." In fact, argued Burger, "[s]ince the Army is sent into territory almost invariably unfamiliar to most soldiers and their commanders, their need for information is likely to be greater than that of the hometown policeman." The Army in this capacity, wrote Burger, "is essentially a police force or a back-up of the local police force," whose power "should be intelligently directed," since "[n]o logical argument can be made for compelling the military to use *blind* force." In other words, if the Army is going to use force to quell domestic disturbances, should it not be allowed to collect as much intelligence as it needs to do so effectively?

These observations, while mostly dicta, were no mere academic speculations on Burger's part. In the summer of 1967, rioting broke out in Detroit after police officers arrested eighty-two people gathered in an unlicensed bar to celebrate the return of two black servicemen from Vietnam. Within a matter of hours, the disturbance went from a bottle thrown at a police car to widespread violence and fires throughout adjacent neighborhoods in the city. By late that afternoon, Detroit's mayor asked for support from the National Guard, and President Johnson ordered federal troops—4,700 paratroopers from the 82nd Airborne Division—to move into the city to restore order. The riots lasted five days, and by the time the last fires were finally extinguished and the soldiers had left, forty-three people had been killed, thirty-three of them African Americans. The experiences in the chaos of the Detroit riots—as well as subsequent disturbances in Watts, California, and Newark, New Jersey—led the Army leadership to reassess its planning process for such contingencies. The problem with gathering intelligence on civilians was made difficult by the "strong resistance of Americans to any military intrusion into civilian affairs," according to Burger. These words reflected the shift in official thinking regarding the use of military force, especially in domestic situations. As prominently displayed during the Ervin Committee hearings, the utterance of the words "national security" was no longer enough to grant the executive branch a blank check to expand its powers. Given this seemingly intractable problem, the Army came up with a solution: keep all such planning secret.

To that end, the Army completed its first such secret civil disturbance plan, code-named Garden Plot, in 1968.[12] The purpose of the plan was to provide a ready-made executive order authorizing the secretary of defense to "take all appropriate steps" to quash civil disturbances. With the president's signature, Garden Plot could be executed and Army troops deployed anywhere "within the 50 states, District of Columbia, Commonwealth of Puerto Rico, US possessions and territories, or any political subdivision thereof" to "[a]id state authorities at the request of the state," "[e]nforce the laws of the United States in any state or territory," and "[p]rotect the civil rights of citizens within a state." The Garden Plot document is a reflection of the times, when civil unrest stemming from racial oppression, political assassinations, the war in Vietnam, and other civil rights protests and demonstrations was occurring on a regular basis, and government authorities were seeking ways not just to react to the disturbances themselves, which were mere symptoms of an underlying problem, but to identify and neutralize the sources of the unrest.

Garden Plot's annex B, titled "Intelligence," went directly to this issue, identifying the likely causes of civil strife the army would face:

> Civil disturbances which are beyond the control of municipal or state authorities may occur at any time. Dissatisfaction with the environment conditions contributing to racial unrest and civil disturbances and dissatisfaction with national policy as manifested in the anti-draft and anti-Vietnam demonstrations are recognized factors within the political and social structure. As such, they might provide a preconditioned base for a steadily deteriorating situation leading to demonstrations and violent attacks upon the social order. The consistency and intensity of these preconditions could lead in time to a situation of insurgency should external subversive forces develop successful control of the situation. Federal military intervention may be required to preserve life and property and maintain normal processes of governments.

This language is a rather unremarkable example of the clash of ideas that naturally occurred as established Cold War thought began to face challenges from within the U.S. citizenry. The growing political opposition movements of the late 1950s and 1960s had become a very real concern for government officials concerned with keeping public order. FBI director J. Edgar Hoover, who saw this as a moral and existential rather than political issue, claimed that the civil rights movement was "spearheaded at times by Communists and moral degenerates."[13] Congress revived the House Un-American Activities Committee (HUAC), a body originally formed in 1938 to investigate the alleged disloyalty and subversion of public officials and private citizens alike, now given new life in the face of civil rights, antiwar, and free speech "subversives."

The public revelations in the late 1960s and early 1970s of military and law enforcement anti-subversive plans and operations made people like the *Tatum* plaintiffs more than a little afraid of government surveillance. For example, under Hoover's personal direction, the FBI had initiated a secret counterintelligence program, code-named COINTELPRO, which began in 1956 as an ongoing operation to "increase factionalism, cause disruption and win defections" within the Communist Party of the United States. Later that same year, Hoover shifted the focus of COINTELPRO to include black civil rights leaders, as he was convinced that the growing civil rights movement was being secretly led by communists. Soon, COINTELPRO was being used to surveil, infiltrate, discredit, and disrupt any group or individual Hoover deemed "subversive," including antiwar protest groups, civil rights groups, the Black Power movement, anticolonialist organizations, feminist groups, churches spreading civil rights or liberation theology messages, and any other entity identifying with the "New Left." Hoover gave COINTELPRO broad powers, both legal and extralegal, to "misdirect, discredit, disrupt and otherwise neutralize" the growing numbers of individuals and groups who fit Hoover's profile as a threat to stability.[14] The methods employed by FBI agents under COINTELPRO expanded the notion of surveillance to include infiltration of groups, psychological warfare and misinformation campaigns, harassment, intimidation, and even violence. The point of COINTELPRO was not to surveil citizens in order to gather evidence for trial, but to conduct illegal break-ins, vandalism, and intimidation to frighten and disrupt activists and their movements. As Hoover himself put it, "[i]t will enhance the paranoia endemic in these circles and will further serve to get the point across there is an FBI agent behind every mailbox."[15] COINTELPRO and other government surveillance programs like it were intended to have a First Amendment chilling effect on their targets. But because the *Tatum* plaintiffs did not (or were not allowed to) present direct evidence of these effects as injury in fact, Chief Justice Burger closed the courthouse doors on them.

The fact that Rehnquist provided the deciding vote for the Court's majority opinion was not lost on the *Tatum* plaintiffs. Without Rehnquist, the decision of the Court would have been 4–4, which would have affirmed the court of appeals decision—granting the *Tatum* plaintiffs standing in this case—and thus allowing the litigation to proceed in the trial court. Senator Ervin, angered by Rehnquist's refusal to follow the example of other similarly situated justices in the Court's history, agreed to draft a public statement criticizing Rehnquist's decision to join the deliberations in a case in which he had a direct interest. After considering the statement for a few days, however, Ervin decided that criticizing a fellow public official would not be consistent with his role as U.S. senator, and opted not to issue the statement.[16] Despite the senator's change of heart, the ACLU decided to move forward with a petition asking for both a rehearing and Rehnquist's recusal from the case, only the second such motion of its kind in the history of the Supreme Court. Ervin approved of the recusal motion, believing that Rehnquist would surely agree to voluntarily withdraw from the proceedings at this point.

The decision by the *Tatum* plaintiffs to file a motion for Rehnquist's recusal was based not on whim, but on long-standing rules for Supreme Court justices. The reasons for such rules are quite obvious: To ensure a court's impartiality, "no man can be a judge in his own case and no man is permitted to try cases where he has an interest in the outcome."[17] In order to achieve as high a degree of impartiality as possible, judges must be hypersensitive to any appearance of bias, even though this "may sometimes bar trial by judges who have no actual bias and who would do their very best to weigh the scales of justice equally between contending parties, . . . [for] justice must satisfy the appearance of justice."[18] While there is case law on this topic, the only statute that directly addresses the recusal of Supreme Court justices is section 455 of the Judicial Code, which, at the time, stated that

[a]ny justice or judge of the United States shall disqualify himself in any case in which he has a substantial interest, has been of counsel, is or has been a material witness, or is so related to or connected with any party or his attorney as to render it improper, in his opinion, for him to sit on the trial, appeal, or other proceeding therein.[19]

Courts had interpreted judicial recusal under this rule to be mandatory, and a justice could use discretion only if the grounds for disqualification had to do with a relationship with a party or their counsel.[20] In addition to the Judicial Code, the American Bar Association maintains its own Code of Judicial Conduct, which, while not binding on justices, is strongly influential as guidelines for the judiciary.

All of these factors combined to convince many, including Ervin, that Rehnquist would agree to recuse himself from the ruling in the face of the *Tatum* plaintiffs' objections. But Rehnquist did not back down. Following the Supreme Court's denial of the plaintiffs' motion for a rehearing on October 10, Rehnquist took the unprecedented step of issuing his own separate memorandum in an attempt to justify his decision to participate in the proceedings.[21] Over sixteen pages, Rehnquist applied a rather legalistic view of the situation, often straining to reach conclusions that seemed to be counter to the principles the Judicial Code was meant to uphold. Rehnquist presented three arguments. First, section 455 of the Judicial Code did not require recusal; second, judicial precedent was on his side; and third, without his participation, the Court would not have been able to break the tie, and the court of appeals decision would stand.

In Rehnquist's first argument, he denied the plaintiffs' claim that he was a formal adviser to the government's legal team in *Tatum*, and could not even be characterized as a material witness in the case, under the meaning of the language in the Judicial Code. He did concede that he could fall under the definition of expert witness for the government as Department of Justice attorney, and he acknowledged that in that role, he had made public statements in which he disagreed with the positions of the *Tatum* plaintiffs, but cited only one direct reference to the case, made during his testimony before the Ervin Committee. In response to the plaintiffs' inclusion of another of his public comments where he directly addressed the issue in *Tatum*, Rehnquist dismissed this as only his personal "understanding of the law on the question of the constitutionality of governmental surveillance," and not a direct reference to the *Tatum* case. In his memorandum, however, Rehnquist left out other instances where he had directly addressed the merits of the *Tatum* case, opining that the *Tatum* plaintiffs were "claiming that others were intimidated [by government surveillance], but really admitting that they were not intimidated at all," and disagreeing that the plaintiffs should be granted standing in a case "to enjoin the gathering of information by the executive branch where there has been no threat of compulsory process and no pending action against any of those individuals on the part of the Government." On this topic, Rehnquist concluded that "[t]he fact that some aspect of [my] propensities may have been publicly articulated prior to coming to this Court cannot, in my opinion, be regarded as anything more than a random circumstance that should not by itself form a basis for disqualification."

Rehnquist next turned to the past actions of other Supreme Court justices under similar circumstances, citing the instances where Justice Hugo Black participated on a case involving the Fair Labor Standards Act despite the fact that he took part in the crafting of that statute, and Justice Felix Frankfurter participated in labor law cases despite the fact that his research while a law professor was concentrated in this field. According to Rehnquist's analysis, "none of the former Justices of this Court since 1911 have followed a practice of disqualifying themselves in cases involving points of law with respect to which they had expressed an opinion or formulated policy prior to ascending to the bench." Further, while "fair minded judges might disagree about the matter," which was a "fairly debatable one," Rehnquist concluded that the applicable statute—referring to the Judicial Code while ignoring the ABA's Code of Judicial Conduct—"does not warrant my disqualification in this case."

Rehnquist concluded his memorandum by reminding everyone that "a federal judge has a duty to *sit* where *not disqualified* which is equally as strong as the duty to *not sit* where *disqualified*." The cases where judges have been disqualified were before district courts and courts of appeals, not the Supreme Court. This was relevant, argued Rehnquist, since

> I think that the policy in favor of the "equal duty" concept is even stronger in the case of a Justice of the Supreme Court of the United States. There is no way of substituting Justices on this Court as one judge may be substituted for another in the district courts. There is no higher court of appeal that may review an equally divided decision of this Court and thereby establish the law for our jurisdiction.

Even if Supreme Court justices were available for substitution, this would not eliminate the very real fact that judges—being human beings—have opinions. To expect otherwise would be not only unrealistic, but also detrimental to the legal process, since "[p]roof that a Justice's mind at the time he joined the Court was a complete *tabula rasa* in the area of constitutional adjudication would be evidence of lack of qualification, not lack of bias."

Finally, Rehnquist pointed out that it was the duty of the Court to resolve difficult constitutional problems such as the one presented in this case. Had he not participated in the proceedings, Rehnquist argued, he would have been derelict in his duty.

> While it can seldom be predicted with confidence at the time that a Justice addresses himself to the issue of disqualification whether or not the

Court in a particular case will be closely divided, the disqualification of one Justice of this Court raises the possibility of an affirmance of the judgment below by an equally divided Court. The consequence attending such a result is, of course, that the principle of law presented by the case is left unsettled. The undesirability of such a disposition is obviously not a reason for refusing to disqualify oneself where in fact one deems himself disqualified, but I believe it is a reason for not "bending over backwards" in order to deem oneself disqualified.

A divided Court, therefore, would leave these difficult questions unsettled, and would be especially damaging in cases where lower courts disagreed as to the proper answers to those questions.

Since one of the stated reasons for granting certiorari is to resolve a conflict between federal courts of appeals, the frequency of such instances is not surprising. Yet affirmance of each of such conflicting results by an equally divided Court would lay down "one rule in Athens, and another rule in Rome" with a vengeance. And since the notion of "public statement" disqualification that I understand respondents to advance appears to have no ascertainable time limit, it is questionable when or if such an unsettled state of the law could be resolved.

Because no litigant is guaranteed "that each judge will start off from dead center in his willingness or ability to reconcile the opposing arguments of counsel with his understanding of the Constitution and the law," Rehnquist argued, his disqualification in this case was improper.

Rehnquist's reasoning on these points rang hollow to the *Tatum* plaintiffs and their counsel. First, Rehnquist's recusal would not prevent the Court from considering the case before it, but would merely give the plaintiffs the opportunity to present their evidence in the district court, and argue their case in that court on its merits. Nothing in a divided Supreme Court decision would prevent the Court from later hearing an appeal of a trial court decision—based on the substantive facts of the case—at a later date. Surely, Rehnquist must have been well aware of the large amount of evidence supporting Article III standing for the *Tatum* plaintiffs, since he had been personally responsible for reviewing much of this evidence in his role as assistant attorney general with the Justice

Department. Second, the examples Rehnquist cites to support his decision to participate in the proceedings felt strained. Justice Frankfurter and Chief Justice Charles Evans Hughes had presided over cases involving topics they had written books about, but those cases had none of the political immediacy of the *Tatum* case. Rehnquist's refusal to recuse himself from this case thus left a point of law unsettled by overstating the effect of split Court decisions on jurisprudence, and muddied the waters around recusal practices, both formal and informal.

So what is the significance of *Laird v. Tatum*? On one level, the decision refused to allow a small group of citizens the opportunity to challenge an Army surveillance program in federal court. But because this decision came from the Supreme Court, its precedential importance resonated beyond the four corners of the *Tatum* plaintiffs' complaint to potentially weaken American citizens' ability to question government surveillance powers. As Justice Douglas wrote in his dissent,

> This case involves a cancer in our body politic. It is a measure of the disease which afflicts us. Army surveillance, like Army regimentation, is at war with the principles of the First Amendment. Those who already walk submissively will say there is no cause for alarm. But submissiveness is not our heritage. The First Amendment was designed to allow rebellion to remain as our heritage. The Constitution was designed to keep government off the backs of the people. The Bill of Rights was added to keep the precincts of belief and expression, of the press, of political and social activities free from surveillance. The Bill of Rights was designed to keep agents of government and official eavesdroppers away from assemblies of people. The aim was to allow men to be free and independent and to assert their rights against government. There can be no influence more paralyzing of that objective than Army surveillance. When an intelligence officer looks over every nonconformist's shoulder in the library, or walks invisibly by his side in a picket line, or infiltrates his club, the America once extolled as the voice of liberty heard around the world no longer is cast in the image which Jefferson and Madison designed.

But how would courts interpret the *Tatum* decision? Was a general rule to emerge from this case, barring plaintiffs generally from challenging secret government surveillance programs? It would not take long to find out.

6

Government Surveillance and the Law

When the Supreme Court handed down its decision in *Laird v. Tatum* on June 26, 1972, it was seeing an early glimpse of a new kind of citizen challenge to government activity. There have always been constitutional challenges, of course. Some of the best-known of the Supreme Court's earliest cases showed a nation and its citizens trying to define just what its government could and could not do under the terms defined by the Constitution. Could individual states tax the federal government?[1] Could Congress wield exclusive legislative power beyond the boundaries of Washington, D.C.?[2] Could a state enforce its laws against Native American nations within its borders?[3] Could the federal government enforce property rights asserted by slave owners over slaves?[4] One can watch the political, social, and economic development of the nation through the questions and challenges its citizens brought against its government. For example, the tensions that led to the outbreak of civil war can be seen in state challenges of federal authority in the 1850s.[5] Similarly, the postwar challenges of Reconstruction in the southern states can be seen through (southern) state actions to limit federal power after the passage of constitutional amendments that protected the rights of all U.S. citizens, including those recently freed from the bonds of slavery.[6] By the 1950s, one can see the beginnings of an increasing willingness among citizens and political groups to challenge laws they alleged were meant only to unconstitutionally preserve the political, social, and economic status quo.[7]

These challenges also addressed the constitutionality of government surveillance, but prior to the introduction of communications technologies such as the telegraph, telephone, and radio, the actions in question concerned physical proximity and manual means. When the telephone began to appear more frequently in individual homes and businesses, law enforcement agencies quickly realized that this relatively new means of communication—which allowed people to hold real-time conversations across previously unimaginable distances—gave them an additional vector for gathering evidence. Such was the case when police in Seattle, Washington, began to take an interest in Roy Olmstead, who they suspected was planning to smuggle liquor into the United States from Canada, which was illegal under the National Prohibition Act. Federal Prohibition agents observed that Olmstead seemed to use telephones located in his home and the homes of his business partners to plan their operations, so they surreptitiously attached additional wires to the telephone lines outside these residences, which allowed them to listen in on all of their telephone conversations.

Olmstead's telephone conversations gave the federal agents everything they wanted and then some. They discovered that not only was Olmstead planning to smuggle liquor into the United States, but he was the general manager of a bootlegging operation that netted $176,000 (nearly $2.5 million in 2016 dollars) per month—and that was only when business was slow. Olmstead employed at least fifty people, operated two oceangoing vessels, owned a ranch outside Seattle with underground storage facilities, and a central office fully staffed with telephone operators, executives, salesmen, deliverymen, dispatchers, scouts, bookkeepers, debt collectors, and an attorney. The magnitude of the Olmstead operation was far beyond the initial expectations of the federal Prohibition agents, who listened in on sales calls that often amounted to two hundred cases of liquor per day. The calls revealed a vast network of fellow conspirators, including members of the Seattle police department, who secured the release of arrested members of the Olmstead organization in exchange for direct payments. The federal agents listened in through the Olmstead phone taps for months, gathering mountains of evidence to make a case in federal court against Olmstead and his co-conspirators. It was a monster of a case.

The *Olmstead* defendants were convicted of conspiring to violate the National Prohibition Act in the District Court for the Western District of Washington on September 21, 1925.[8] The defendants appealed the decision before the Ninth Circuit Court of Appeals, which affirmed the district court's decision on May 9, 1927.[9] They then appealed the decision to the Supreme Court, which granted certiorari on one question: whether the use in evidence of private telephone conversations, intercepted by means of wiretapping, violated the Fourth and Fifth Amendments.[10]

The relevance of *Olmstead v. United States*, however, rested on what, exactly, a "search" was under the language of the Fourth Amendment.

The Fourth Amendment to the U.S. Constitution provides that "[t]he right of the people to be secure in their persons, houses, papers, and effects against unreasonable searches and seizures shall not be violated; and no warrants shall issue but upon probable cause, supported by oath or affirmation and particularly describing the place to be searched and the persons or things to be seized." Courts have wrestled with the exact meaning of this language since it was first drafted, and the interpretations of the courts over the nation's history track the changing legal and social landscape through time. For example, in the 1842 case of *Prigg v. Pennsylvania*, the Supreme Court held that since the Constitution guaranteed the right of a slave owner to seize a slave, it followed that the federal government had the authority to enforce that right, despite the language of the Fourth Amendment.[11] The Court in *Ex parte Jackson* (1877), where the defendant had been indicted for sending illegal materials through the U.S. mail service, held that the Fourth Amendment extends to letters and sealed packages subject to letter postage in the mail.[12] In *Boyd v. United States* (1886), the Court observed that Fourth Amendment protections do not require actual entry upon a premises and search for and seizure of papers to constitute an unreasonable search and seizure, a detail that would later be relevant to *Olmstead*.[13]

In the early twentieth century, Fourth Amendment doctrine assumed the need for government agents to physically trespass upon the suspect's property before their actions could be qualified as a search under the Fourth Amendment. This makes sense when one considers that at the end of the nineteenth century, the home telephone was still in relative infancy and the concept of remotely searching or seizing anything was considered fanciful (or, more accurately, not considered at all). It was with this doctrine in mind that the *Olmstead* Court took note in the fifth paragraph of its majority opinion that the federal Prohibition agents tapped Olmstead's lines "without trespass upon any [of his] property" by attaching their wires to telephone lines on public streets outside his home and offices. *Boyd*, which seemed to stray from current Fourth Amendment trespass doctrine, was the first case the Court considered. While Chief Justice William Howard Taft, writing for the majority, agreed that the *Boyd* Court indeed had held that a Fourth Amendment search had taken place without trespass, he distinguished that case from the facts before the *Olmstead* Court by noting that the government in *Boyd* had made an official demand for the papers, where the federal Prohibition agents had not demanded any information from Olmstead. The Court looked to *Ex parte Jackson*, as well, but wrote that federal agents passively listening in on phone taps had nothing in common with the opening of sealed envelopes and packages in the U.S. mail. Taft observed that the federal Prohibition agents neither compelled nor induced the *Olmstead* defendants to talk on their telephones—"[t]hey were continually and voluntarily transacting business without the knowledge of interception." Taft wrote that "[t]he well known historical purpose of the Fourth Amendment . . . was to prevent the use of governmental force to search a man's house, his person, his papers and his effects . . . against his will," so a Fourth Amendment search must "be of material things." Further, "[t]he United States takes no such care of telegraph or telephone messages as of mailed sealed letters." Taft found that none of the cases cited held that the Fourth Amendment could be violated "unless there has been an official search and seizure of his person, or such a seizure of his papers or his tangible material effects, or an actual physical invasion of his house," and therefore, the wiretapping of Olmstead "did not amount to a search or seizure within the meaning of the Fourth Amendment."

One of the more interesting facets of our system of jurisprudence is the concept of the dissenting opinion. Why, one might wonder, would we care about the opinions of judges who disagree with the majority? After all, it is the majority—or in some cases, the plurality—opinion that gives rise to the court's judgment in a case. While it is true that dissenting opinions do not create binding legal precedent, they can be cited by courts in subsequent cases as persuasive authority, and have provided some of the basis for overturning past precedents. In fact, some cases are better known for their dissents than for their majority opinions. Take the infamous 1856 Supreme Court decision in *Dred Scott v. Sandford*, for example.[14] In *Scott*, a slave from Missouri whose master had brought him north into what is now Minnesota, where slavery was illegal, sued for his freedom and the freedom of his wife and daughters, arguing that their four years spent in free territories gave them that right. The majority opinion in *Scott*, penned by Chief Justice Roger Taney, a Jacksonian

Democrat and a strong believer in states' rights, held that not only did Dred Scott not have the right to his and his family's freedom, but African Americans had no right to sue in U.S. courts since they were not, nor could they ever be, citizens of the United States. While the Taney opinion is well known, the two scathing dissents from Justices John McLean and Benjamin Curtis became lightning rods to northern abolitionists, and helped form the basis for the Thirteenth, Fourteenth, and Fifteenth Amendments passed after the Civil War. Similarly, the Supreme Court in *Plessy v. Ferguson* (1896), where an "octoroon" (the term used at the time for people who were seven-eighths white and one-eighth black) named Homer Plessy had been arrested in Louisiana for sitting in an all-white train car, held that his arrest did not violate the Constitution under the "separate but equal" doctrine.[15] Justice John Harlan's dissent in this case, where he firmly stated that "[i]n respect of civil rights, all citizens are equal before the law," which "regards man as man and takes no account of his surroundings or of his color," became the basis for the Court's unanimous decision in *Brown v. Board of Education* fifty-eight years later.[16]

The dissent in *Olmstead*—authored by Justice Louis Brandeis—is another such example. Prior to his appointment to the Supreme Court, Brandeis was known for, among other things, one of the first articulations in U.S. legal thought of the concept of the "right to privacy," in an 1890 *Harvard Law Review* article of the same name.[17] He had also built a reputation as the "people's lawyer," devoting his time to fighting monopolies, defending labor laws, and earning the nickname "a Robin Hood of the law" from the *Economist* newspaper. In 1916 President Wilson nominated Brandeis as associate justice to the Supreme Court. His nomination was immediately contested by conservative Republicans within the government, including Chief Justice Taft, who objected to Brandeis's progressive "radicalism" and said that he was "unfit" to serve on the Court. Based almost solely on Wilson's endorsement, Brandeis's nomination was confirmed in the Senate on June 1, 1916, by a vote of forty-seven to twenty-two. In his early years as a member of the Court, Brandeis was relatively quiet, weighing in on railroad injury cases and employment and labor cases. In the years immediately following World War I, however, the United States became increasingly conservative and isolationist, a trend reflected in the laws and cases that came before the Supreme Court. In 1919, for example, the Supreme Court considered the case of defendants accused of printing antiwar pamphlets forbidden under the Espionage Act of 1917.[18] A majority upheld the defendants' conviction under the act, but Brandeis, in his dissent, included in the record the entire text of the pamphlet in question and asserted,

> The fundamental right of free men to strive for better conditions through new legislation and new institutions will not be preserved, if efforts to secure it by argument to fellow citizens may be construed as criminal incitement to disobey the existing law—merely, because the argument presented seems to those exercising judicial power to be unfair in its portrayal of existing evils, mistaken in its assumptions, unsound in reasoning or intemperate in language.

Later that same year, the Court considered a case from the Minnesota Supreme Court, which had affirmed the defendant's conviction for violating a Minnesota statute that made it illegal to interfere with or discourage the enlistment of men into the U.S. armed services.[19] The U.S. Supreme Court upheld the Minnesota Supreme Court's decision, declaring the Minnesota statute valid under the U.S. Constitution. Justice Joseph McKenna, writing for the majority, stated that while the freedom of speech "is natural and inherent, . . . it is not absolute, [and] it is subject to restriction and limitation." McKenna reminded the reader that "[t]he Nation was at War with Germany" and the defendant's "speech was the discouragement of that." This war "was not declared in aggression, but in defense, in defense of our national honor," and "[i]t would be a travesty on the constitutional privilege [the defendant] invokes to assign him its protection." As he did in his dissent in *Pierce*, Brandeis vigorously disagreed with the majority opinion here, writing that the Minnesota statute was in his opinion invalid "because it interferes with federal functions and with the right of a citizen of the United States to discuss them." By protecting the Minnesota statute, and others like it, by declaring them constitutional, the Court was protecting acts that "prevent teaching that the abolition of war is possible" by abridging freedoms of speech and of the press "not in a particular emergency, in order to avert a clear and present danger, but under all circumstances." In his concluding paragraph, Brandeis considered the Minnesota statute in light of the Fourteenth Amendment, which guarantees that "no State shall make or enforce any law which shall abridge the privileges or immunities of citizens of the United States." Addressing this amendment—but likely speaking for constitutional rights generally—Brandeis wrote, "I cannot believe that the liberty guaranteed by the Fourteenth Amendment includes only liberty to acquire and to enjoy property."

Given his strong support for constitutional civil liberties, it should come as no surprise that Brandeis's dissent in *Olmstead* has become one of the best-known examples of a minority opinion overshadowing the majority's ruling in Supreme Court history. He began by briefly recounting the facts concerning the wiretaps. But rather than focus on the physical location of the wires used by the federal Prohibition agents, he looked at the results of their use. The government

> tapped eight telephones, some in the homes of the persons charged, some in their offices. Acting on behalf of the Government and in their official capacity, at least six other prohibition agents listened over the tapped wires and reported the messages taken. Their operations extended over a period of nearly five months. The type-written record of the notes of conversations overheard occupies 775 typewritten pages.

For a government activity that did not amount to a "search" under the Fourth Amendment (according to the majority opinion), it managed to collect a great deal of evidence that, but for the telephone, would have otherwise required the sort of invasive search that would have required a warrant. Indeed, observed Brandeis, the government did not attempt to defend the methods used to wiretap Olmstead, and conceded "that if wire-tapping can be deemed a search and seizure within the Fourth Amendment, such wire-tapping as was practiced in the case at bar was an unreasonable search and seizure." But according to the government's arguments, the protections articulated in the Fourth Amendment "cannot properly be held to include a telephone conversation." Clearly, the government—and the Supreme Court majority—was missing the constitutional forest for the semantic trees.

As Brandeis reminded the Court,

> When the Fourth and Fifth Amendments were adopted, the form that evil had theretofore taken, had been necessarily simple. Force and vio-

lence were then the only means known to man by which a Government could directly effect self-incrimination. It could compel the individual to testify—a compulsion effected, if need be, by torture. It could secure possession of his papers and other articles incident to his private life—a seizure effected, if need be, by breaking and entry. Protection against such invasion of the sanctities of a man's home and the privacies of life was provided in the Fourth and Fifth Amendments by specific language.

But, wrote Brandeis, the language used by the drafters of the Constitution and its amendments was necessarily limited by the worlds that they knew. Just because the Founders had not yet conceived of the concept of remotely communicating with one another over a copper wire did not mean that the protections intended in these amendments must be contextually frozen in time. Brandeis observed that

> time works changes, brings into existence new conditions and purposes. Subtler and more far-reaching means of invading privacy have become available to the Government. Discovery and invention have made it possible for the Government, by means far more effective than stretching upon the rack, to obtain disclosure in court of what is whispered in the closet.

The Constitution, wrote Brandeis, "undertook to secure conditions favorable to the pursuit of happiness," which "recognized the significance of man's spiritual nature, of his feelings and of his intellect." The authors of the Constitution "sought to protect Americans in their beliefs, their thoughts, their emotions and their sensations." Perhaps most importantly, "[t]hey conferred, as against the Government, the right to be let alone—the most comprehensive of rights and the right most valued by civilized men."

It is difficult for those of us reading Brandeis's words today to fully appreciate just how radical the concept of individual privacy was for its time. In fact, it would take many decades before courts began to truly understand and accept privacy as a legal—and not just a social—concept. Many of the building blocks for the concept were present in the relatively young political theories of republicanism and constitutional democracy, as well as in the ancient common law theories of libel and trespass, but the idea that individual citizens might have a general right to be left alone by their government as well as by their fellow citizens was as modern as the technology that helped spur its articulation—the camera, the rapid adoption of which in the late nineteenth century had begun to make people nervous about its capability of erasing what had been an invisible border around our private lives. The recognition by Brandeis of the importance of privacy not only to healthy societies, but also to healthy democracies, put his thinking many decades ahead of its time.

Brandeis argued that such an important and fundamental right cannot be preserved by simply protecting an individual's person and property, stating that it is "immaterial where the physical connection with the telephone wires leading into the defendants' premises was made." Further, such an intrusion is not made more acceptable merely because it "was in aid of law enforcement." Channeling the revolutionary enthusiasm of the nation's founders, Brandeis wrote,

> Experience should teach us to be most on our guard to protect liberty when the Government's purposes are beneficent. Men born to freedom are naturally alert to repel invasion of their liberty by evil-minded rulers. The greatest dangers to liberty lurk in insidious encroachment by men of zeal, well-meaning but without understanding.

These words were a direct challenge from Brandeis to the Court's majority, asking them to consider their opinion in the context of the Constitution's aims and intents, and not merely satisfy themselves with a rote understanding of the document's words. As with his other well-known dissents, Brandeis reserved his most damning language for the final paragraph:

> Decency, security and liberty alike demand that government officials shall be subjected to the same rules of conduct that are commands to the citizen. In a government of laws, existence of the government will be imperilled if it fails to observe the law scrupulously. Our Government is the potent, the omnipresent teacher. For good or for ill, it teaches the whole people by its example. Crime is contagious. If the Government becomes a lawbreaker, it breeds contempt for law; it invites every man to become

a law unto himself; it invites anarchy. To declare that in the administration of the criminal law the end justifies the means—to declare that the Government may commit crimes in order to secure the conviction of a private criminal—would bring terrible retribution. Against that pernicious doctrine this Court should resolutely set its face.

These sentiments were quite shocking in the context of the 1928 Supreme Court, but were early signals of the political and social change to come. Under Chief Justice Taft, the Supreme Court had steered a conservative course, limiting the ability of the federal government to regulate private business and industry, resisting attempts to end child labor, and curtailing freedom of speech, especially when it ran against the interests of government. Taft also expanded the role of chief justice during his tenure on the Court, and took on a managerial role over the associate justices, urging them to maintain unanimity and discouraging dissents. In this respect, Brandeis was a perpetual thorn in Taft's side, and in some ways, confirmed Taft's misgivings about his initial appointment to the Court. Over time, however, Taft developed a grudging respect for Brandeis, acknowledging him as a hard worker on the bench.

Despite Brandeis's impassioned defense of civil liberties in his dissent, the *Olmstead* majority opinion would remain as Fourth Amendment doctrine for nearly four decades. During this period—from the years immediately following World War I through the years following the even greater devastation of World War II—the U.S. federal government steadily expanded its role in many areas, including military preparedness and the intelligence infrastructure that accompanied it. Before the United States entered World War I in 1917, the military took little notice of Germany as a potential enemy. The war in Europe had long been an increasingly bloody stalemate by that time, and military leaders in the Wilson administration, fearing the eventual spread of the war into the Americas, began to push for additional power—and funds—to increase military intelligence-gathering capabilities and strengthen domestic security operations. For example, Brigadier General Montgomery Macomb, then chief of the Army's War College Division, urged President Wilson to endorse plans for military-directed censorship of civilian communications, by martial law if necessary, to prevent the publication of any material that might "prove detrimental to national defense or useful to a possible enemy."[20] This sentiment grew stronger within military circles as another world war loomed in the 1930s, this time with federal law enforcement agencies in tow. When J. Edgar Hoover was summoned to the White House to meet with President Roosevelt to discuss foreign espionage in 1936, he came prepared with a plan based on years of his experiences leading the Bureau of Investigation (reorganized as the Federal Bureau of Investigation in 1935) and framed by his personal conviction that the nation must increase its protections against enemy espionage, counterespionage, sabotage, and subversive activities. This important job, Hoover argued, must include the FBI, and Roosevelt agreed, ordering Hoover to send him all information on American individuals and organizations suspected of "subversive activities." The order did not bother to define what activities might be seen as "subversive," but instead gave general instructions to keep a close eye on communists, fascists, or any other individual or group who advocated the "overthrow or replacement of the government of the United States." Hoover's FBI now had a national security mission to collect intelligence domestically.

Hoover was not particularly interested in investigating pro-fascist and other right-wing elements, and instead directed the bulk of his agency's efforts toward members of the Communist Party, labor organizations and leadership, and other citizens and groups that fit Hoover's personal definition of "subversive." The biggest question he faced with this task was how federal law enforcement agents had been using the *Olmstead* decision as a judicial green light to continue the practice of non-trespassory wiretapping until 1934, when Congress passed the Federal Communications Act, section 605 of which prohibited the interception of conversations.[21] This was not a blanket prohibition, however, and the FBI chose to interpret section 605 as prohibiting only those wiretaps that were "divulged." That is, wiretaps were not illegal if the information gained from them was not used as evidence in court. Wiretaps became an important tool in the FBI's kit. Hoover's FBI also noted that agents could easily expand the scope of legal surveillance methods using the same strategy they employed on section 605. That is, if the FBI did not intend to publicly divulge the information gained through surveillance as evidence in court, who was to say what was allowed under the law? Under this interpretive umbrella, the FBI added bugging and breaking-and-entering ("black bag jobs") to its domestic surveillance repertoire.

Following the end of World War II, the FBI's domestic surveillance programs were briefly curtailed by the Truman administration's concern that it was "building up a Gestapo" in the United States. As an increasingly powerful Soviet Union emerged as a new threat, however, Cold War concerns over the nation's nuclear secrets gave the FBI renewed permission to continue—and expand—its domestic surveillance programs.

The postwar increase in government surveillance activity did not go unnoticed, especially in light of the still-vivid memories of the horrific results of repressive governments. In surveillance cases before the Supreme Court in the late 1940s and 1950s, the Court began to reassert the importance of the Fourth Amendment as a necessary—if sometimes inconvenient—component of a constitutional democracy, one that was to be interpreted and enforced by courts, and not by overreaching law enforcement agencies or officers. In *McDonald v. United States* (1948), for example, the Court wrote that Fourth Amendment protections are not mere "formalities," nor are they intended to "shield criminals nor to make the home a safe haven for illegal activities," but served instead the "high function" of "interpos[ing] a magistrate between the citizen and the police."[22] Justice William O. Douglas, writing for the majority, stated that "[t]he right of privacy was deemed [by the Founders] too precious to entrust to the discretion of those whose job is the detection of crime and the arrest. Power is a heady thing; and history shows that the police acting on their own cannot be trusted. And so the Constitution requires a magistrate to pass on the desires of the police before they violate the privacy of the home." Similarly, in *Johnson v. United States* (1948), Justice Robert H. Jackson wrote,

> The point of the Fourth Amendment, which often is not grasped by zealous officers, is not that it denies law enforcement the support of the usual inferences which reasonable men draw from evidence. Its protection consists in requiring that those inferences be drawn by a neutral and detached magistrate instead of being judged by the officer engaged in the often competitive enterprise of ferreting out crime. Any assumption that evidence sufficient to support a magistrate's disinterested determination to issue a search warrant will justify the officers in making a search without a warrant would reduce the Amendment to a nullity and leave the people's homes secure only in the discretion of police officers. Crime,

even in the privacy of one's own quarters, is, of course, of grave concern to society, and the law allows such crime to be reached on proper showing. The right of officers to thrust themselves into a home is also a grave concern, not only to the individual but to a society which chooses to dwell in reasonable security and freedom from surveillance. When the right of privacy must reasonably yield to the right of search is, as a rule, to be decided by a judicial officer, not by a policeman or government enforcement agent.[23]

This jurisprudential trend reached its zenith in 1967, in yet another case involving wiretapping by federal law enforcement agents, where the Supreme Court abandoned the Fourth Amendment trespass doctrine that had been in place since its 1928 decision in *Olmstead*. The case of *Katz v. United States* had its beginnings in early 1965, when the FBI began to suspect Charles Katz of operating an illegal gambling operation.[24] The FBI watched Katz as he used the same set of three public telephone booths at the same time of day, almost on a daily basis. These observations alone were not enough to establish probable cause for a warrant, however. It did not take long for FBI agents to formulate a plan that would allow them to collect enough evidence against Katz to convince a judge that a warrant could be issued: they would simply place microphones on the top of the telephone booths Katz used. There was no need to drill holes through the booths' walls, nor any need to cut and splice wires. Under the Fourth Amendment trespass doctrine, they argued, there was no search, and therefore no need for a warrant.

In late February 1965, FBI agents went through with their plan, placing microphones on top of two of the telephone booths Katz regularly used, and, with the help of the telephone company, placed the third booth out of order.[25] In addition to bugging the telephone booths, an FBI agent rented the apartment next door to Katz and listened to his conversations through their shared wall without the aid of electronic devices (a glass or stethoscope may have been enough in this case). These methods would not, of course, allow the FBI agents to listen to both sides of Katz's telephone calls. But they were able to hear Katz say things like "I have Northwestern minus 7," and "Oregon plus 3," and "Don't worry about the line. I have phoned Boston three times about it today"—all of which were used to convince a judge that the FBI had probable cause to serve as the basis for a warrant to search Katz's apartment and belongings for harder evidence of bookmaking and gambling.

During the subsequent trial, the FBI produced the materials its agents had seized from their search of Katz's apartment, and Katz objected to their use as evidence, arguing that the basis for the original warrant—the notes and logs from the FBI agents' bugging of the telephone booths—constituted an illegal search and seizure under the Fourth Amendment. Both the trial court and the Court of Appeals for the Ninth Circuit disagreed with Katz's argument, so he looked to the Supreme Court to consider the following two constitutional questions:

1. Whether the public telephone booth is a constitutionally protected area, so that evidence obtained by attaching an electronic listening recording device to the top of such a booth is obtained in violation of the right to privacy of the user of the booth; and
2. Whether physical penetration of a constitutionally protected area is necessary before a search and seizure can be said to be violative of the Fourth Amendment to the Constitution.

The Supreme Court granted certiorari, but disagreed with Katz's formulation of the issues. First, the Court stated that "the correct solution of Fourth Amendment problems is not necessarily promoted by incantation of the phrase 'constitutionally protected area.'" Second, the Court disagreed that the Fourth Amendment could be "translated into a general constitutional 'right to privacy.'" Instead, the Court observed that the Fourth Amendment's "protections go further, and often have nothing to do with privacy at all." Disposing with these traditional interpretations of Fourth Amendment doctrine, which had at least tacitly been in place long before *Olmstead*, the Court boldly held that "the Fourth Amendment protects people, not places," and held that the FBI agents had performed a warrantless (and therefore, illegal) search when they placed the microphones on top of the public telephone booths.

Perhaps the most important words from *Katz*, however, did not appear in the Court's majority opinion. In his brief concurring opinion, Justice Harlan asserted that "a person has a constitutionally protected reasonable expectation of privacy." This phrase would become the new standard against which Fourth Amendment cases were to be decided. Harlan explained his reasoning further:

> As the Court's opinion states, "the Fourth Amendment protects people, not places." The question, however, is what protection it affords to those people. Generally, as here, the answer to that question requires reference to a "place." My understanding of the rule that has emerged from prior decisions is that there is a twofold requirement, first that a person have exhibited an actual (subjective) expectation of privacy and, second, that the expectation be one that society is prepared to recognize as "reasonable." Thus a man's home is, for most purposes, a place where he expects privacy, but objects, activities, or statements that he exposes to the "plain view" of outsiders are not "protected" because no intention to keep them to himself has been exhibited. On the other hand, conversations in the open would not be protected against being overheard, for the expectation of privacy under the circumstances would be unreasonable.

By the time the Supreme Court handed down its decision in *Laird v. Tatum* on June 26, 1972, the nation was generally far less accepting of secret (and illegal) domestic surveillance by its own government. Challenges to government military and law enforcement intelligence programs were increasingly finding their way into the news media, political debates, and federal courts. A watershed moment in this debate took place in the Supreme Court just the week before the *Tatum* decision was handed down, in a case that pitted the federal government against the U.S. District Court for the Eastern District of Michigan.[26] This case began as a criminal prosecution of three defendants—John Sinclair, Lawrence Plamondon, and John Forrest—for conspiring to destroy federal government property. The three defendants were leaders of the White Panther Party, a far-left radical group that advocated "cultural revolution" and anti-racist activities. The group was active in the Detroit and Ann Arbor areas, and became well known throughout the country (especially since Sinclair also managed the band MC5). In December 1969, the three were indicted in connection with the 1968 bombing of a Central Intelligence Agency office in Ann Arbor. On October 5, 1970, the defendants filed a pretrial "Motion for Disclosure of Electronic or

Other Surveillance, for a Pre-trial Hearing, to Suppress Evidence and to Dismiss the Indictment." The government filed a response in opposition to the defendants' motion on December 18, and included an affidavit from the U.S. attorney general, John Mitchell. In his affidavit, Mitchell acknowledged that at least one of the defendants' conversations had been bugged or wiretapped, but argued that the logs from this surveillance were to be given as a sealed exhibit for *in camera* (within the judge's chambers) inspection only. District court judge Damon Keith heard briefing and oral arguments on the motion and reply on January 16, 1971. On January 25, Judge Keith held that the electronic surveillance by the government had been illegal and ordered the government to disclose all information on the wiretaps and bugging sought by the defendants.

The government immediately appealed Keith's decision to the Sixth Circuit Court of Appeals, arguing that all wiretaps in this case had been personally approved by Attorney General Mitchell, and any public revelation of the government's electronic surveillance in this case would "prejudice the national interest."[27] The question before the court of appeals was "[w]here the Attorney General determines that certain wiretaps are 'necessary to protect the nation from attempts of domestic organizations to attack and subvert the existing structure of government,' does his authorization render such wiretaps lawful without judicial review?" The government argued that in cases of national security, the president, in his capacity as chief executive, "has unique powers of the 'sovereign' which serve to exempt him and his agents from the judicial review restrictions of the Fourth Amendment." In other words, the government argued that the recent paradigm shift in Fourth Amendment doctrine brought about through the Court's decision in *Katz* was irrelevant when it comes to presidential decisions regarding the security of the nation: "This power is the historical power of the sovereign to preserve itself."

The Sixth Circuit Court of Appeals acknowledged the "eloquent and breathtaking" sweep of presidential powers set forth in the Constitution, but noted that the government identified "no suggestion of limitations on such power" in its brief. Further, the court noted that the Constitution offered no grant of power to the president to make searches and seizures without regard for the Fourth Amendment, and pointed to the

1952 case of *Youngstown Sheet & Tube Co. v. Sawyer*, where President Truman had seized control of privately held steel mills to avoid a nationwide steel strike, arguing that this action was "within his inherent power as Chief Executive charged with seeing that the laws are 'faithfully executed.'"[28] The Supreme Court rejected this argument, holding that such actions were a job for Congress, not for military or executive authorities, for "if the President had authority to issue the order he did, it must be found in some provisions of the Constitution." No such provision can be found. The Sixth Circuit acknowledged that *Youngstown* was not a case about wiretapping, but it was highly relevant to the case before it because it dealt directly with the inherent powers of the presidency, which went to the real question before them: Can the president ignore the Fourth Amendment—or, by extension, other constitutional provisions—under the umbrella of "national security"? The Sixth Circuit thought not, holding that "in dealing with the threat of domestic subversion, the Executive Branch of the government, including the Attorney General and the law enforcement agents of the United States, is subject to the limitations of the Fourth Amendment to the Constitution when undertaking searches and seizures for oral communications by wire." The government, dissatisfied with this analysis, appealed its case to the Supreme Court, which granted certiorari on June 21, 1971.

The case before the Supreme Court, now known also as the *Keith* case after the Eastern District Court judge presiding over the original proceedings, addressed "the delicate question of the President's power, acting through the Attorney General, to authorize electronic surveillance in internal security matters without prior judicial approval." The Court acknowledged that this question was "a matter of national concern, requiring sensitivity both to the Government's right to protect itself from unlawful subversion and attack and to the citizen's right to be secure in his privacy against unreasonable Government intrusion." But it was also careful to point out "the limited nature of the question before the Court," and emphasized that the case "raises no constitutional challenge to electronic surveillance specifically authorized by Title III of the Omnibus Crime Control and Safe Streets Act," which had been passed by Congress in 1968 and authorized use of electronic surveillance for a specific list of crimes, subject to a prior court order. In addition, the Court observed that there is no "question or doubt as to the necessity of obtaining a warrant in the surveillance of crimes unrelated to the national security interest." The question before the Court, therefore, was a narrow one, addressing a question left open by *Katz*: "[w]hether safeguards other than prior authorization by a magistrate would satisfy the Fourth Amendment in a situation involving the national security."

Faced with such a fundamental question regarding the surveillance powers of the president, the Court began with constitutional first principles. After acknowledging the powers and duties of the president to provide for the security of the nation and its citizens, the Court echoed the nation's growing discomfort with increasing government surveillance, observing that the "recognition of these elementary truths does not make the employment by Government of electronic surveillance a welcome development." While national security issues raise both First and Fourth Amendment questions, the Court looked to the nation's origins, stating that "Fourth Amendment protections become the more necessary when the targets of official surveillance may be those suspected of unorthodoxy in their political beliefs." The dangers of abuse by an overzealous government agency or agent were quite real, and examples of which are to be found in abundance. The Court stated,

> The price of lawful public dissent must not be a dread of subjection to an unchecked surveillance power. Nor must the fear of unauthorized official eavesdropping deter vigorous citizen dissent and discussion of Government action in private conversation. For private dissent, no less than open public discourse, is essential to our free society.

The protections articulated by the Fourth Amendment could not, therefore, be guaranteed if questions regarding the appropriateness of domestic surveillance were left solely to the discretion of the executive branch of government. And while there are exceptions to the Fourth Amendment's warrant requirement, it was "[b]eyond doubt that the First Amendment is the cornerstone of American freedom. The Fourth Amendment stands as guardian of the First."

Justice Lewis Powell, writing for the majority, upheld the Sixth Circuit's opinion, holding that "the Government's concerns [over national security] do not justify departure in this case from the customary Fourth Amendment requirement of judicial approval prior to initiation of a search or surveillance." Powell acknowledged that "some added burden will be imposed upon the Attorney General" from this conclusion, but such "inconvenience is justified in a free society to protect constitutional values." But the Court was also quite careful to articulate the exact boundaries of the scope of its decision. First, it restated that its holding applied only to domestic aspects of national security, and did not address activities of foreign powers or agents. The Court acknowledged that national security concerns were different from those of "ordinary crime," and acknowledged that "the emphasis of domestic intelligence gathering is on the prevention of unlawful activity or the enhancement of the Government's preparedness for some possible future crisis or emergency. Thus, the focus of domestic surveillance may be less precise than that directed against more conventional types of crime." The Court was not attempting "to detail the precise standards for domestic security warrants any more than our decision in *Katz* sought to set the refined requirements for the specified criminal surveillances which now constitute Title III." It held simply that "prior judicial approval is required for the type of domestic security surveillance involved in this case."

At the time of the Supreme Court's decision in *Tatum*, the nation as a whole appeared to be questioning government overreach justified by Cold War or other retrograde policies that did not appear to be working, either internationally or domestically. The individuals behind these policies did not generally impose them with bad intentions, but as Justice Brandeis wrote in his *Olmstead* dissent, "The greatest dangers to liberty lurk in the insidious encroachment by men of zeal, well-meaning but without understanding." Did the Court's decision in *Tatum* run counter to this fundamental philosophy? More importantly, how would subsequent surveillance challenges in U.S. courts fare with respect to Article III standing? The *Tatum* plaintiffs were not the only parties wishing to have their day in court, and they all wished to see whether Justice Douglas's dissent in *Tatum* could become the next *Olmstead*-ian lever toward fundamental change in American jurisprudence.

7

The Legacy of *Laird v. Tatum*

Within a few weeks of the Supreme Court's decision in *Tatum*, federal courts were beginning to apply *Tatum* as precedent to deny standing to plaintiffs seeking to challenge government surveillance and related programs. Cases before the Courts of Appeals for the D.C. Circuit, the Fourth Circuit, and the Seventh Circuit were dismissed for lack of standing, applying the *Tatum* decision.[1] The courts in these cases recognized in *Tatum* the emergence of a rule wherein the mere existence of a subjective "chilling effect" on plaintiffs from government surveillance did not present the objective harm, or threat of specific future harm, required by Article III standing doctrine. This question was one of increasing relevance to U.S. courts in the mid-1970s, when ninety-five challenges to government surveillance were brought before the federal bench from 1972 to 1976, nine of these making it all the way to the Supreme Court for a final decision.

These cases did not emerge from nowhere, of course. By the mid-1970s, American citizens had become aware of an alarming number of surveillance abuses by their government, and were pressing their congressional representatives to do something about it. Hearings on military surveillance and the multiple revelations that came out of the Nixon administration's Watergate scandal convened by Senator Ervin convinced Congress to pass the Federal Privacy Act in 1974, which limited the gathering, storage, and use of citizen data by federal agencies, requiring each such agency to

> maintain no record describing how any individual exercises rights guaranteed by the First Amendment unless expressly authorized by statute or by the individual about whom the record is maintained or unless pertinent to and within the scope of an authorized law enforcement activity.[2]

In *Donohoe v. Duling* (1972), for example, the Court of Appeals for the Fourth Circuit considered a case wherein citizens had challenged the

Richmond, Virginia, police department's surveillance practices, citing their chilling effects on protected political activities. The *Donohoe* plaintiffs offered as evidence the "routine" practice by the Richmond police of surveilling public demonstrations and political meetings where uniformed officers would take photographs of the participants, and would use this information to establish internal files, which they offered, on request, to other law enforcement agencies. The city of Richmond defended this program as "acceptable police practice throughout the country to record demonstrations, both peaceful and otherwise" based on law enforcement's "need to know who the leaders (of the demonstrations) are," and asserted that the plaintiffs had no standing to bring this action since they had not demonstrated any injury resulting from the police department's actions.

The only testimony from a plaintiff in the case came from Douglas Donohoe, the named plaintiff in the action, who stated that he had attended a meeting on the campus of Virginia Commonwealth University in Richmond, and witnessed police officers taking photographs of everyone entering the meeting. It turned out, however, that the officers Donohoe saw outside the meeting were not from the Richmond police department, but were security personnel employed by the university. These officers were not connected with the Richmond police, nor were they under their direction or control. The defendants acknowledged the surveillance of demonstrations and meetings, but asserted that the plaintiffs had failed to show any actual injury due to any activity by the Richmond police.

Much like the Court in *Tatum*, the *Donohoe* court found the plaintiffs' continued attendance at multiple demonstrations and meetings to run counter to their complaint that their First Amendment rights had been "chilled" in any real sense of the word. The court pointed out that the plaintiffs had provided detailed evidence of multiple instances of police surveillance and photography, and yet the plaintiffs continued to attend these events. "At best," the court observed, "[the plaintiffs] asserted that they were 'annoyed,' or 'felt uncomfortable,' or 'nervous,'" which did not "establish harm or injury actually sustained by the plaintiffs themselves." The court pointed to the plaintiffs' supporting testimony that "frankly conceded that nothing the Richmond police authorities did induced them to desist from their prominent roles in public demonstrations or meetings." Rather, "[t]heir only complaint was that others were not as forthright or courageous as they; they claimed the right to speak for these more timorous individuals." The court, citing *Tatum*, held that "the 'chilling' effect of executive actions, falling short of a direct restraint of First Amendment rights, would not give rise to a justiciable cause if it arose merely from the individual's knowledge that a governmental agency was engaged in certain activities or from the individual's concomitant fear that, armed with the fruits of those activities, the agency might in the future take some other and additional action detrimental to that individual." As such, the *Donohoe* court found that the plaintiffs,

> undeterred by any action by the defendants and offering no testimony of injuries done to him (them)—of any inhibiting of their own exercise of the rights of free speech, of any penalty imposed on them which could be attributed to their exercise of their First Amendment rights, of any loss of employment or even reasonably foreseeable threat of such, of any threat of prosecution, or specific, identifiable civil sanction—seek primarily in this action to vindicate the alleged rights of others, whose actual intimidation or injury is purely conjectural and speculative, without any positive proof in support, and were therefore without standing to bring their claim.

Other courts took a more expansive view of the *Tatum* decision. In *Handschu v. Special Services Div.*, for example, the District Court for the Southern District of New York observed that, following *Tatum*, "[t]he use of informers and infiltrators by itself does not give rise to any claim of violation of constitutional rights."[3] In *Fifth Ave. Peace Parade Committee v. Gray*, the court considered plaintiffs' allegations that, among other surveillance activities, the FBI had asked for—and received—a plaintiff's bank records, including deposit amounts, signature cards, and names of individuals associated with the plaintiff's account.[4] The plaintiffs argued that the circumstances in *Tatum* were distinguishable from the facts of their case, since the *Tatum* plaintiffs had presented a "general challenge to the existing system of military surveillance of civilian activities," whereas in the instant case, their "claim [of] intrusion was specific since it related to particular acts of Government agents." The court rejected this argument, stating that the plaintiffs had alleged "mere speculative apprehension of future misuse of information and hence no objective harm and no justiciable issue."

Some courts, however, applied the *Tatum* decision to find standing for plaintiffs based on the notion that, if plaintiffs offering facts like those presented in *Tatum* did not meet the standing doctrine's threshold requirement of actual injury, plaintiffs whose evidence of injury appeared more substantial would meet that standard. The question for post-*Tatum* courts thus became one of degree: Where, exactly, was the line that separated surveillance plaintiffs who deserved Article III standing from those who would be shown the courthouse door? In *Philadelphia Resistance v. Mitchell*, for example, plaintiffs had, under the rules governing pretrial discovery, filed a motion to compel responses from the federal government defendants in their complaint alleging harassment by government officials.[5] The defendants responded that the information the plaintiffs sought was privileged because it concerned an ongoing criminal investigation. The defendants also objected to the plaintiffs' questions on the grounds that they lacked standing to obtain the information in the first place. After privately examining the defendants' proposed answers to the plaintiffs' interrogatories, the court agreed that the defendants could assert a claim of privilege. The court balked, however, at the defendants' assertion that, under *Tatum*, the plaintiffs had failed to show that they had standing to bring their claims. The *Philadelphia Resistance* court held that the plaintiffs in the present case were

> challenging much more than mere Army surveillance which was described by the circuit court merely as good newspaper reporting. Rather, they allege that the government has conducted excessive surveillance involving physical violence, threats, illegal searches and seizures, illegal electronic surveillance and the denial of the right to counsel.

The court thus ordered the government defendants to answer a subset of the plaintiffs' interrogatories, and the case to proceed.

Other courts were willing to follow this pattern, allowing more specific allegations of First Amendment "chill" than those found in *Tatum* as sufficient to support standing. In *Alliance to End Repression v. Rochford*, the U.S. District Court for the Northern District of Illinois was faced with what it termed "a broadbased attack on allegedly unlawful intelligence gathering activities of the Intelligence Division of the Chicago, Illinois, Police Department."[6] In their complaint, the *Alliance* plaintiffs challenged "a vague and overbroad mandate contained within a general order of the Chicago Police Department directing its Intelligence Division to gather intelligence on organizations and individuals who pose 'a threat to the security of the country, state or city.'" The plaintiffs' allegations included a wide array of police surveillance activities, including

> (1) surveillance and intelligence-gathering on individuals and organizations engaged in lawful activities; (2) unlawful wire-tapping and other forms of electronic surveillance; (3) unlawful entry and seizure; (4) dissemination of derogatory information concerning plaintiffs; (5) summary punishment and harassment; and (6) infiltration of private meetings and political organizations by informers and provocateurs.

These activities, the plaintiffs claimed, had "the effect of chilling, harassing and disrupting [their] exercise of their First Amendment rights." The defendants responded with a motion to dismiss the plaintiffs' case, citing *Tatum* as a basis to assert "that plaintiffs have no standing to seek injunctive relief because the plaintiffs have alleged no more than a subjective 'chill' of their rights and that such allegations are insufficient to sustain [their] complaint." The *Alliance* court disagreed with the defendants, however, finding that

> the complaint in the instant case reveals that the allegations contained therein differ greatly from those contained in the *Laird* case and that, consequently, the decision in *Laird* is inapposite to the instant suit. The plaintiffs in the case at bar have alleged that they were the specific objects of both overt and covert surveillance on the part of the defendants. The plaintiffs' claims contain assertions that defendants specifically impinged upon their constitutional rights through various types of activities as outlined below.

The *Alliance* court thus denied the defendants' motion to dismiss the case.

The Supreme Court itself was soon faced with the vexing line-drawing problem it had tacitly constructed in *Tatum*. Just a few months after its decision in *Tatum*, the Court was faced with a complaint brought by the Socialist Workers Party and others, who asserted that government officials had interfered with their political activities, and sought injunctive relief.[7] The district court in the case granted a preliminary injunction to the plaintiffs, which barred government agents and their informants from attending or otherwise monitoring the national convention of the plaintiffs' youth organization. On an expedited appeal from the government defendants, the U.S. Court of Appeals for the Second Circuit vacated most of the district court's injunction, while still prohibiting the government's transmitting of the names of persons attending the convention, pending the final determination of the case. The plaintiffs then sought a stay of the Second Circuit's judgment and a reinstatement of the district court's original injunction.

The question the *Socialist Workers Party* Court was forced to consider was the threshold matter posed by the plaintiffs' action: Upon which side of the *Tatum* Article III standing line did the plaintiffs in the instant case fall? Much like the *Tatum* plaintiffs, the *Socialist Workers Party* plaintiffs had complained of government surveillance activities that had had a "general chilling effect" on their First Amendment rights. But the *Socialist Workers Party* Court observed that the *Tatum* plaintiffs' "chill" arose out of their "distaste for the Army's assumption of a role in civilian affairs or from their apprehension that the Army might at some future date misuse the information in some way that would cause direct harm to [them]," which was not enough to support standing in that case. In the present case, however, the Court found the plaintiffs' allegations "much more specific," with the government activity having "the concrete effects of dissuading some [plaintiff] delegates from participating actively in the convention and leading to possible loss of employment for those who are identified as being in attendance." Whether or not these claims were enough to survive on the merits was not relevant—the question was one of standing to bring the claims in the first place. The Court held that the level of specificity of injury in the plaintiffs' claims was sufficient, under *Tatum*, to grant Article III standing.[8] This distinction drawn by the *Socialist Workers Party* Court was somewhat puzzling, and appeared to narrow the broad view of *Tatum* as a high bar to surveillance cases.

The key to locating this line for courts, therefore, was to decide just when a complaint contained more than a mere "subjective chill" to a plaintiff's First Amendment rights. But what allegations must a plaintiff bring before a court before that line was crossed, and standing could be granted? As a foundation, *Tatum* stood for the proposition that "subjective chill" arising from a general system of public surveillance, data gathering, and dissemination, absent some additional form of harassment, was not enough. The *Donohoe* court would not grant standing where police had conducted surveillance of demonstrations, public vigils, and meetings, and had taken photographs of the attendees. Plaintiffs' allegations of warrantless FBI searches of bank and transportation records were not enough to meet the standing requirement. Was there even such a thing (as far as the courts were concerned) as a cognizable injury to First Amendment rights based on political surveillance without some articulable evidence of bad faith on the part of the government defendants?

In 1975 Senator Frank Church and Representative Otis Pike formed committees in the Senate and House, respectively, to review and report on government surveillance abuses, establishing permanent intelligence oversight committees in the next congressional session. On January 29, 1976, Pike's House Select Intelligence Committee issued its final report, and on April 26, the Church Committee issued its report, both recommending limits on domestic surveillance activities.[9] Even the executive branch felt compelled to evaluate its own activities, when President Gerald Ford, having recently assumed the office of the presidency following the August 9, 1974, resignation of Richard Nixon, created the Rockefeller Commission on CIA Activities within the United States. In 1978 the Foreign Intelligence Surveillance Act (FISA) was passed, which directly addressed the issues raised by the Pike and Church Committees, as well as the surveillance questions raised by the *Keith* case.

These tensions between citizens and government over aggressive domestic surveillance programs were on full display in cases like *Jabara v. Kelley*, which was decided by the District Court for the Eastern District of Michigan in 1979.[10] Abdeen Jabara was an attorney in Detroit, and was active in multiple Arab clubs and organizations. In 1967 the FBI began surveilling Jabara, and continued that surveillance through December 1975. The motives for the FBI's investigation of Jabara were unclear. While there had been one early aspect of its surveillance that had to do with a criminal investigation, the entire record of its activities failed to show any evidence linking Jabara to the commission (or the anticipated commission) of any crime whatsoever. The FBI's surveillance was quite extensive, including physical surveillance by FBI agents as well as informants, the inspection of Jabara's bank records, warrantless electronic surveillance by both the FBI and the NSA, interviews with third parties, and the dissemination of information gained during the investigation. The surveillance method most preferred by the FBI during this investigation was the use of informants who reported on Jabara's political activities, including his attendance at various public and private political gatherings. The FBI's informant would usually supplement this information with a summary of Jabara's discussions during those meetings. When asked by the court for a justification of the eight-year surveillance of Jabara, the FBI asserted a "legitimate national security investigation."

One of the critical questions facing the *Jabara* court was that of standing, and how the *Tatum* decision should be interpreted and applied to the facts in this case. The government defendants in *Jabara* asserted that *Tatum*, and the subsequent cases that followed *Tatum*, supported their argument that Jabara had no standing to bring his case before a federal court, asserting that the plaintiff had only articulated "allegations of a subjective 'chill,'" which did not meet the *Tatum* standard of injury supporting Article III standing. The court disagreed, stating that Jabara's

> allegations of a system of independently unlawful intrusions into his life
> as the result of his lawfully held and lawfully expressed political views is
> sufficient to take the chilling effect which he alleges outside the realm of
> speculation and subjectivity. Unlike *Tatum* this is not a case where the
> plaintiff is attacking a general system of intelligence gathering. Nor can
> the Court say that, as in *Tatum*, the chill alleged by Jabara results from the
> mere knowledge that he is being investigated.

Perhaps key to the court's skepticism regarding *Tatum*'s applicability to Jabara's case was the fact that he

> alleges that not only has he felt fear at expressing his political views, but
> that others have been deterred from associating with him because of the
> FBI investigation. Not only this, but the plaintiff alleges that false and

misleading reports of his activities have been accumulated by the FBI and disseminated to other federal agencies and foreign governments. In addition, Jabara has alleged injury to his reputation and legal business as the result of publicity surrounding the FBI investigation of him.

Based on this reasoning, the *Jabara* court denied the defendants' motion to dismiss the case for lack of standing, and went on to grant summary judgment and injunctive relief to Jabara on his Fourth and First Amendment claims.

The *Jabara* court's decision regarding the plaintiff's standing to challenge government surveillance revealed the exposed nerve that made this issue such a sensitive one: If executive branch agencies choose to monitor a citizen's political activities for national security reasons and under otherwise legal conditions, can the judiciary allow those who are monitored to challenge (and possibly halt) this surveillance on the basis that their mere knowledge of it somehow "chilled" their First Amendment activities? Federal law enforcement agencies saw this as an improper trespass by one branch of government into another's legal sphere. This separation of powers problem rarely is the primary focus in courts, yet remains a lingering background question whenever the judiciary is asked to examine (or alter) the activities of the executive. In the *Keith* case, for example, the Court observed that the "judicial role accords with our basic constitutional doctrine that individual freedoms will best be preserved through a separation of powers and division of functions among the different branches and levels of Government," but that only "prior review by a neutral and detached magistrate" of some executive activities such as surveillance would provide the "time-tested means of effectuating Fourth Amendment rights." Besides, it had become increasingly apparent throughout the 1970s that the executive branch had for some time been abusing the rather long surveillance leash that separation of powers doctrine had granted it, the NSA's noteworthy (and first-time) admission that it had been spying on an American citizen in the *Jabara* case providing one more example to that long list.

Thus, when the government defendants in *Jabara* appealed that court's decision, the separation of powers argument was not expressly articulated, but it could be read between every line of their brief to the Sixth Circuit Court of Appeals, which challenged the district court's decision granting Jabara summary judgment on his Fourth and First Amendment claims.[11] Critical to Jabara's claim was the exact mechanism by which the FBI obtained information through the warrantless electronic surveillance of him. In 1971 the FBI, likely lacking sophisticated electronic eavesdropping capabilities, asked the NSA to conduct this warrantless surveillance on the FBI's behalf. In its analysis, the court of appeals went directly to an earlier justification of NSA domestic surveillance activities by the Court of Appeals for the D.C. Circuit, which stated that the

> NSA itself has no need for intelligence information; rather, it is a service organization which produces intelligence in response to the requirements of the Director of Central Intelligence. The mission of the NSA is to obtain intelligence from foreign electrical communications. Signals are acquired by many techniques. The process sweeps up enormous numbers of communications, not all of which can be reviewed by intelligence analysts. Using "watch-lists"—lists of words and phrases designed to identify communications of intelligence interest—NSA computers scan the mass of acquired communications to select those which may be of specific foreign intelligence interest. Only those likely to be of interest are printed out for further analysis, the remainder being discarded without reading or review. Intelligence analysts review each of the communications selected. The foreign intelligence derived from these signals is reported to the various agencies that have requested it. Only foreign communications are acquired, that is, communications having at least one foreign terminal.[12]

This antiseptic description of the NSA's activities makes the agency seem to operate at arm's length, and the *Jabara* appeals court seized upon it. Because Jabara failed to contend in his briefs that the NSA violated his Fourth Amendment rights during this surveillance, the appeals court therefore took "as a given that the information was legally in the hands of the NSA." The question then became whether there was a Fourth Amendment violation when the FBI received the intercepted communications from the NSA. The court ultimately agreed that, while Jabara may have had a *subjective* expectation of privacy in his overseas communications, the court doubted that an *objective* expectation existed when one government agency lawfully obtains information and then shares it with another agency. The appeals court ended up vacating the lower court's judgments, but on grounds that did not touch on a *Tatum* standing analysis, which still suffered from a lack of clarity.

Unfortunately, the courts' analysis of the standing doctrine in surveillance cases only got muddier as the turbulence of the mid-1970s gave way to the 1980s. One of the chief causes of this confusion arose out of the government's use of the state secrets privilege. This privilege, like other such privileges restricting the introduction of certain information as evidence, gives its user the right to foreclose evidence from a court, even if the evidence foreclosed from discovery may show the violation of constitutional or other rights by the government. For this reason, courts have observed that this privilege is "not to be lightly invoked," and its use "must be carefully considered to assure that the proper balance is struck between the interest of the public and the litigant in vindicating private rights and the public's interest in safeguarding of the national security."[13]

The contemporary understanding of the state secrets privilege largely originated in the 1953 case of *United States v. Reynolds*, which was a claim by the widows of three civilian observers killed in the crash of an Air Force B-29 airplane.[14] During discovery, the *Reynolds* plaintiffs sought to obtain the official U.S. Air Force report on the crash as well as statements made by the surviving crew members taken during the government's official inquiry into the accident. The government defendants in the case refused to provide this information on the basis that it was barred from public disclosure by Air Force regulations. The district court rejected the government's claim of secrecy, after which the secretary of the Air Force filed a formal claim of privilege, which explained to the court that the flight in question in *Reynolds* involved the testing of electronic equipment and other items that were "highly secret" and could not be disclosed to the court "without seriously hampering national security, flying safety and the development of highly technical and secret military equipment." The district court rejected these arguments as well, and the government defendants appealed the decision to the U.S. Court of Appeals for the Third Circuit, which affirmed the lower court's decision. The government then appealed its case to the Supreme Court, which granted certiorari in *Reynolds* to answer "the important question of the Government's privilege to resist discovery."

In its briefing before the *Reynolds* Court, the government argued that the executive branch may withhold documents from courts if it is in the "public interest." The Court acknowledged the existence of such a privilege, based in part on the separation of powers doctrine, but pointed out that while the "privilege against revealing military secrets . . . is well established in the law of evidence," judicial understanding of the scope of this privilege was limited, and established three broadly worded procedural steps necessary to invoke the state secrets privilege. First, since the privilege belonged to the government, no private party can claim or waive the privilege. Second, the privilege is not to be "lightly invoked." Third, the state secrets privilege must be formally invoked by the chief of the department in control of the matter after "actual personal consideration of that officer." The power to decide whether such a claim of state secrets privilege was appropriate was given to the courts, which must make the decision "without forcing a disclosure of the very thing the privilege is designed to protect." A court's analysis of the claim would depend on a balancing test that would use a "showing of necessity" (of government disclosure) as its unit of measure. Even if the plaintiffs could present a strong showing of necessity in favor of the government's release of the information in question, however, the court could overrule the plaintiffs' claim if it was "ultimately satisfied that military secrets are at stake."

The *Reynolds* Court's procedural rules gave the judiciary a great deal of discretion in the evaluation of the invocation of the state secrets privilege, which might give courts cause to request an *in camera* review of the government documents in question in order to better assess their claim of privilege. Not so fast, said the *Reynolds* Court, which explicitly denied automatic review of government documents by the court, reasoning that "[i]t may be possible to satisfy the court, from all the circumstances of the case, that there is a reasonable danger that compulsion of the evidence will expose military matters which, in the interest of national security, should not be divulged," even to the Court itself. This "reasonable danger" test added a layer of confusion to the *Reynolds* test. For example, how could a judge, likely not an expert in the nature of the presumed military secrets, properly scrutinize the government documents in question with an eye toward "reasonable danger"? On top of that, how much deference was a court supposed to give to a government claim that the information in question posed a "reasonable danger" of risk if exposed? The "reasonable danger" test thus confused the distinction between an evaluation of the sensitivity of the information and a determination that the information in question is indeed present in the evidence.

When the *Reynolds* Court applied this test to the case at hand, it upheld the government defendants' claim of state secrets privilege in the matter, observing that the plaintiffs had alternative evidence available to them that they should have used in order to avoid a confrontation with the government over privilege. The Court did not dismiss the plaintiffs' complaint, however, instead remanding the case back to the district court, thus allowing the plaintiffs to continue the pursuit of their claim (without the official government reports of the accident). Rather than pursue their claims, the plaintiffs settled with the government for a sum of $170,000, releasing the defendants from liability in the matter.[15]

The state secrets privilege collided with *Tatum*'s interpretation of standing to challenge surveillance programs in 1982, in *Halkin v. Helms*.[16] *Halkin* was the culmination of years of litigation brought by twenty-one individuals and five organizations against the heads of the CIA, FBI, Department of Defense, Secret Service, and others, claiming that their domestic surveillance activities in the late 1960s and early 1970s violated the plaintiffs' rights under the First, Fourth, Fifth, and Ninth Amendments, among other claims. The plaintiffs brought their original action in 1975 after the Rockefeller Commission on CIA Activities within the United States revealed the fact that government agencies had conducted domestic surveillance operations of U.S. citizens who opposed the Vietnam War. The plaintiffs, all of whom were actively protesting the war and calling for an end to U.S. involvement in Southeast Asia in the 1960s and early 1970s, argued that these surveillance activities were unconstitutional.

The two surveillance programs that ended up as the focus of this litigation were the CIA's Operation CHAOS and the NSA's ongoing practice of scanning electronic communications on behalf of the CIA, FBI, and Secret Service. The rather comically named Operation CHAOS was a CIA intelligence program to determine the extent to which foreign governments were exerting domestic influence through their support of individuals and groups critical of the Vietnam War. CHAOS was initiated in 1967 during the Johnson administration and was led by CIA director

Richard Helms and executed by the CIA's newly formed Special Operations Group. Through CHAOS operations, the CIA produced a number of reports on its ongoing analysis of the domestic antiwar movement, and presented these reports to the White House, the FBI, and other government agencies. The program began by physically and electronically surveilling Americans who were identified as part of the antiwar community as they traveled abroad. In 1969, however, CHAOS began using agents to infiltrate domestic antiwar groups, supplying information on their activities to the CHAOS database. The NSA actively assisted in the CHAOS program, providing communications surveillance based on "watch lists" and keywords compiled by the CIA's Special Operations Group. From 1967 to 1973 the CIA, FBI, Secret Service, and defense agencies submitted names of people and organizations to the NSA for electronic surveillance, ultimately collecting data on more than a thousand American citizens.

In the initial action before a D.C. district court, the secretary of defense, one of the named defendants, asserted a claim of state secrets privilege on behalf of the U.S. government. The district court agreed, and on appeal, the Court of Appeals for the D.C. Circuit agreed with the lower court, holding that the NSA was not required to confirm in discovery whether or not it had actually intercepted any of the plaintiffs' communications.[17] Without this evidence, however, the plaintiffs were left without a way to prove their claims, and their case was thus dismissed. Despite this setback, the plaintiffs renewed their case against the CIA and other individuals and agencies who submitted the watch lists to the NSA for later search and interception of the plaintiffs' communications. They would soon run into additional obstacles on this front, as well, chief of which was the continued problem of discovery. For example, when the plaintiffs requested information and documents relating to the conduct of Operation CHAOS, the CIA declined to supply all of the information requested, on grounds of the state secrets privilege, among other objections. The district court again agreed with the government's claim, and the *Halkin* plaintiffs once again appealed this decision.

The *Halkin* court was therefore called upon to evaluate the application of the state secrets privilege once more, with the fate of the plaintiffs' Article III standing under *Tatum* again in jeopardy. Again, the court of appeals agreed with the lower court's decision, and holding that, without sufficient evidence of cognizable injury, the plaintiffs lacked standing to bring their case. This chicken-and-egg reasoning was necessary, explained the *Halkin* court, since although "there can be little doubt that the complaint alleged facts—interception of plaintiffs' private communications—which if proved would constitute an injury in fact, [and would permit] plaintiffs to go forward in an effort to prove the truth of those allegations and any consequent liability of the defendants," their case could not proceed because "evidence of the fact of acquisition of plaintiffs' communications by NSA cannot be obtained by the government [under the state secrets privilege], nor can such fact be presumed from the submission of watchlists to that Agency." Thus, following the *Tatum* requirement that plaintiffs must show "either a specific present objective harm or a threat of specific future harm" to be granted standing, the *Halkin* court held that "the absence of proof of actual acquisition of [plaintiffs'] communications is fatal to their watchlisting claims." But surely, argued the plaintiffs, this reasoning endangers most challenges to secret government surveillance programs, especially those conducted in the name of national security. Besides, was it not more likely than not that the plaintiffs' communications had been targeted by the defendants, given what was publicly known about Operation CHAOS? The court responded by observing that even if the plaintiffs' probabilistic claims were true, it would "add[] nothing to their case. The fact that an individual is more likely than a member of the population at large to suffer a hypothesized injury, while perhaps lending support to his standing to complain, makes the injury no less hypothetical."

The Court of Appeals for the D.C. Circuit doubled down on this precedent again in October 1982, when thirty-six plaintiffs, including the United Presbyterian Church, challenged the constitutionality of Executive Order 12333, signed by President Ronald Reagan on December 4, 1981, establishing "the framework in which our governmental and military agencies are to effectuate the process of gathering foreign intelligence and counterintelligence information, and the manner in which intelligence-gathering functions will be conducted at home and abroad."[18] The *United Presbyterian* plaintiffs argued that the order was "unconstitutionally vague, authorizes intrusions upon their constitutionally protected rights, and 'chills' the exercise of their rights of free expression and exercise of religion." The court of appeals, echoing the familiar strain that emerged from the *Tatum* decision that took a dim view of plaintiffs who "appear to be seeking a judicial determination of the constitutionality of the entire national intelligence-gathering system," cited *Halkin* to deny standing. Since the *United Presbyterian* plaintiffs could not access evidence that they were surveilled under Executive Order 12333, "they [had] not adequately averred that any specific action is threatened or even contemplated against them," and even if a probabilistic argument were allowed on the part of plaintiffs, "that would still fall far short of the 'genuine threat' required to support [*Tatum's*] theory of standing."

Thus, the cases that applied and developed *Tatum's* legacy of standing doctrine were creating jurisprudence that appeared to set a very high bar indeed to plaintiffs seeking to challenge secret government surveillance. In fact, courts were establishing precedent that created a "damned if you do, damned if you don't" type of obstacle to plaintiffs asserting First Amendment chill from government surveillance. Even if plaintiffs could demonstrate to a court that they more probably than not were subjects of government surveillance, that alone was insufficient to establish standing under *Tatum*. The doctrine that was taking shape put surveillance plaintiffs into two categories. The first category was made up of those who asserted harms due to the chilling effect on their First Amendment or other rights. The second category included plaintiffs who argued that they were injured due to a loss of privacy from the government's surveillance efforts. Both categories of plaintiff faced serious obstacles to establishing standing in federal courts under *Tatum* and its progeny. Those who assert chilling effects often have plentiful evidence of the actual surveillance program, from such sources as newspaper accounts, congressional hearings, or leaked documents. But according to *Tatum*, a general "chill" alone does not satisfy the requirements for standing. Conversely, plaintiffs who argue that their injuries were due to a loss of privacy will generally have no difficulties convincing a court that such injuries confer standing, but will have difficulties producing evidence of the actual surveillance activities due to such doctrines as the state secrets privilege. The frequency of such challenges began to wane in the late 1980s and early 1990s, as a nation stepped back from a Cold War footing, and Americans, exhausted by government scandal, washed their hands of the Vietnam/Watergate era. But as the relatively peaceful period following the Cold War began to give way to an era of increased threats of terrorism, government leaders began the process of reinvigorating the nation's intelligence infrastructure. Where would *Tatum* jurisprudence fit in such a changing world? A heretofore unimaginable tragedy would soon spark two wars and a global surveillance renaissance, forcing U.S. courts to answer this question once again.

8

Technology, National Security, and Surveillance

When the Foreign Intelligence Surveillance Act (FISA) was signed into law in 1978, it represented years of anger and frustration from U.S. citizens arising out of multiple revelations of government overreach and corruption, and their insistence that Congress act to provide legislative and judicial oversight over future executive actions to assure Americans that the abuses of the past would not be repeated. Specifically, FISA emerged from the Supreme Court's decision in the *Keith* case, requiring domestic surveillance programs to adhere to Fourth Amendment principles, and the many public disclosures of surveillance abuses that emerged through the efforts of the Ervin Committee, the Pike Committee, and the Church Committee. FISA, along with a number of related surveillance reforms, was seen as an agreed-upon balance between the branches of government, with the executive conceding some amount of oversight of its intelligence activities, and the legislative and judicial branches agreeing to perform most of this oversight out of public view, through the use of secret court warrant proceedings.

For those who harbored suspicions about FISA's effectiveness in reining in government surveillance abuses, there were questions about the use of FISA regulations and the secret FISA court as a rubber stamp to approve all—or nearly all—warrant applications the government might produce. These concerns were not without basis. Between 1979 and 2003, only three out of over sixteen thousand government applications for warrants were actually denied by the FISA court. These objections, however, remained in the minority during the prosperous and mostly peaceful era that stretched through the late 1980s and early 1990s. During this period, government surveillance activity had significantly ebbed, with only a few hundred warrant applications presented each year. By the mid-1990s, however, the executive branch began agitating for increased surveillance powers based on two primary concerns—technology and terrorism.

By the 1980s, computers were beginning to show up in a rapidly increasing number of homes, classrooms, and offices, although they were mainly used as standalone devices at the time. As networking and communications technologies caught up, however, the era of ubiquitous computing saw its dawn. Regional telephone companies, left over from the 1982 breakup of AT&T, began laying fiber optic cables everywhere they could. The esoteric network once known as the ARPANet began to expand beyond the universities and research labs that had nurtured it to life over the past decade or so, and took on a new name—the Internet—that has since become so universally recognized and generic that journalists are beginning to change the uppercase *I* to lowercase. In 1991 a physics researcher at the European Organization for Nuclear Research (CERN) named Tim Berners-Lee developed a protocol for encoding, linking, and sharing information that quickly became the basis for what became known as the World Wide Web. Communications researchers began taking advantage of these technological advances, developing new technologies such as Voice Over IP (VoIP), which allowed one to place telephone calls over digital networks, and video compression and streaming protocols. In a word, the world was going digital, and government law enforcement and intelligence agencies were becoming concerned that many of their surveillance methods would soon become obsolete.

As this pace of technological advancement quickened, the FBI lobbied Congress for updated surveillance laws to keep up in this new digital world. In 1994 Congress responded with the Communications Assistance for Law Enforcement Act (CALEA), a law that would require all U.S. telecommunications companies to build special access interfaces for government use, regardless of their underlying technologies. The government asked for more changes as cell phone networks began to explode and VoIP use was routing more and more telephone calls over the Internet, which was not included within the scope of CALEA's language. A compromise solution was reached in which VoIP systems that were centrally managed were fair game under CALEA.

During this same period, Americans were developing an increased sense of unease regarding the threat of terrorist attacks on U.S. soil. The concept of terroristic violence in the United States was not a new one, of course. Following the end of the Civil War, the late nineteenth century was an era of severe growing pains for the nation, when questions over racial equality, labor rights, and the many other issues arising from the relatively rapid advances in industrialization and the beginnings of globalization often resulted in violence. One of the earliest uses of terror as a weapon in these struggles was by segregationists and white supremacists, mainly (but certainly not exclusively) in southern states, where lynchings, bombings, and arson became tragically common occurrences. Clashes between business and labor also created an environment where terror became useful. For example, in May 1886, workers in Chicago took part in a nationwide strike, with over eighty thousand workers taking to the streets in protest of working conditions and wages. Among these striking workers were anarchists and other revolutionaries who were agitating for changes that went far beyond labor conditions to an overthrow of the capitalist system as a whole. A protest rally was held in Haymarket Square on May 4, where the striking workers gathered to hear speeches from a number of national labor leaders. When Chicago police moved in to disperse the crowd, a homemade bomb made from dynamite in a thin metal casing was thrown toward the advancing officers. When it exploded, the shock and shrapnel ended up killing seven police officers and at least four protesters, with dozens of others injured by the blast. The early twentieth century saw many more such bombings, often carried out by anarchist groups with similar goals to those involved in the Haymarket bombing. Racially motivated terror attacks continued well into the twentieth century. In 1963, four members of the Ku Klux Klan planted over a dozen sticks of dynamite attached to time-delay fuses in the basement of the 16th Street Baptist Church, an African American church in racially segregated Birmingham, Alabama. Birmingham had seen many instances of segregationist violence before this, with over twenty bombings of the city's black churches and businesses in the decade before 1963. The bombs went off on the morning of Sunday, September 15, killing four girls who were changing into their choir robes before services, and injuring twenty-two others. These examples of domestic terror had sparked varying levels of panic among citizens in the years immediately following the events, sometimes resulting in government surveillance policies that were later shown to be unconstitutional. Events of the 1990s would begin this cycle once more.

On February 26, 1993, a Kuwaiti citizen named Ramzi Yousef and his Jordanian friend Eyad Ismoil drove their rented Ryder van containing a

1,500-pound bomb made from highly explosive fertilizer into the parking garage beneath the World Trade Center in New York City. Yousef and Ismoil lit the bomb's fuse and left the garage. The bomb went off twelve minutes later, creating a hundred-foot hole through four levels of concrete, knocking out power to the buildings, and filling the stairwells and elevator shafts with thick black smoke. Six people were killed in the aftermath, with over a thousand others injured. Just over two years later, Timothy McVeigh and Terry Nichols, both Americans, used the same technique on a larger scale—a 5,000-pound fertilizer bomb in the back of a rented truck—to destroy the Alfred P. Murrah Federal Building in Oklahoma City, killing 168 people and injuring over 680 others. And in 1996, during the Summer Olympic Games held that year in Atlanta, three pipe bombs packed with masonry nails went off in the crowded Centennial Olympic Park, killing two and injuring over a hundred others. The people behind these acts of terror had very different motivations behind their crimes, but to the U.S. military, intelligence community, and law enforcement agencies, it meant that they needed more leeway in conducting surveillance domestically.

But from 1978 to the end of the 1990s, the FISA compromise between the executive, legislative, and judicial branches of government appeared to be largely unchangeable. The legal and political structures that formed FISA appeared to be working to the satisfaction of most, with only a very few claims of First Amendment chill or loss of privacy showing up in U.S. courts. Indeed, the separation FISA created between foreign intelligence surveillance and domestic law enforcement, articulated in and around the clause requiring that "the purpose of the surveillance is to obtain foreign intelligence information," meant that domestic law enforcement agencies could not perform an end run around the Fourth Amendment by obtaining warrants through the secret FISA court. In 1976 U.S. Attorney General Edward Levi issued the Guidelines on Domestic Surveillance to the FBI and other federal law enforcement agencies, which limited domestic security investigations to activities that both "involve or will involve the use of force and violence," and "involve or will involve the violation of federal law." These guidelines required the FBI to report on all investigations, and required that all such investigations "shall be designed and conducted so as not to limit the full exercise of rights protected by the Constitution and laws of the United States."

Following the troubling acts of domestic terrorism in the 1990s, however, federal law enforcement agencies began looking for ways to expand their access to surveillance through FISA. Courts were beginning to recognize a broadening of the FISA language, allowing domestic surveillance where "the primary purpose" rather than "the [sole] purpose" of the surveillance was to obtain foreign intelligence. The legislative branch was also becoming more willing to listen to the FBI's requests. For example, while FISA had originally applied only to electronic surveillance, Congress agreed to expand its scope to include other, more traditional law enforcement tools, including physical searches, telephone pen registers and trap-and-trace orders, and the search of business records. Perhaps the most significant sign of change in the use of FISA for domestic surveillance can be found in the sharp spike in FISA orders issued from the mid-1990s onward, as illustrated in figure 8.1. But the legal and political dimensions of domestic surveillance activities that had formed the understanding between the branches of government (and its citizens) since 1978 would be rendered unrecognizable after the events of late 2001.

Within a few short hours on the morning of September 11, 2001, four coordinated terrorist attacks in New York City, Washington, D.C., and western Pennsylvania had killed 2,996 people, injured over 6,000 oth-

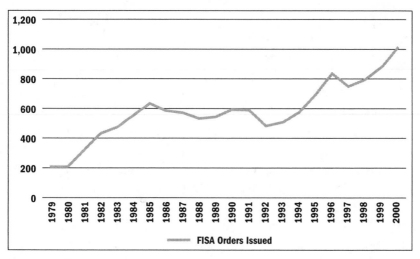

Figure 8.1. FISA orders issued, 1979–2000. Electronic Privacy Information Center, Foreign Intelligence Surveillance Act Court Orders, 1979–2015.

ers, and caused over $10 billion in property damage, with $3 trillion in overall costs. Almost immediately, the Bush administration initiated multiple efforts to expand government anti-terror efforts, including a proposed bill that would, among other things, suspend the writ of habeas corpus indefinitely.[1] The executive branch applied a significant amount of political pressure on Congress to pass its proposed measures as quickly as possible, and the legislative houses bypassed their usual committee conferences, sending bills directly to up-or-down votes, even going so far as to sanction a congressman who attempted to initiate debate around portions of the act. When some legislators began to question the corrosive effect the proposed Homeland Security Act would have on constitutional civil liberties, Attorney General John Ashcroft had this to say to them:

> To those who scare peace-loving people with phantoms of lost liberty, my message is this: your tactics only aid terrorists, for they erode our national unity and diminish our resolve. They give ammunition to America's enemies, and pause to America's friends. They encourage people of good will to remain silent in the face of evil.

The message from the Bush administration was clear: Until this crisis passes, it is not an appropriate time to debate the niceties of constitutional values. In fact, those who do are at best, distracting, and at worst, unpatriotic or possibly seditious.

Perhaps the most sweeping legislation to come out of the aftermath of 9/11 was the 2001 USA PATRIOT Act, which made two significant changes to FISA.[2] First, it allowed applications to the FISA court for warrants where foreign intelligence was only "a significant purpose" rather than the sole purpose of the investigation. Second, it gave government agencies the ability to collect physical objects—not just electronic intelligence—as part of their surveillance program. These changes poked large holes in the traditional separation between law enforcement and intelligence gathering that was a keystone of FISA until that time. Attorney General Ashcroft issued internal guidelines to this effect, which authorized investigations even if the intelligence purposes of the surveillance were secondary to the criminal investigative purposes. This caused even the secretive FISA court to object. In May 2002 the FISA court published its first public opinion, protesting Ashcroft's internal guidelines. The court held that the separation between law enforcement and intelligence gathering needed to be reestablished, pointing out the very real possibility for abuse. In September 2000, for example, the government admitted that it made "misstatements and omissions of material facts" in seventy-five of its applications to the FISA court. The FISA court argued that if the wall between criminal law enforcement and foreign intelligence gathering was not reestablished, the system could be gamed by federal prosecutors and law enforcement agents:

> [C]riminal prosecutors will tell the FBI when to use FISA (perhaps when they lack probable cause for Title III electronic surveillance), what techniques to use, what information to look for, what information to keep as evidence, and when use of FISA can cease because there is enough evidence to arrest and prosecute.

But even the FISA court was not immune to the pressures being applied by the Bush administration. The government appealed the FISA court's decision, arguing that, among other things, the order violated separation of powers doctrine and "exceed[ed] the constitutional authority of Article III judges." A three-judge appellate court ended up reversing the lower FISA court's ruling, making the novel observation that FISA was not meant to apply only to foreign intelligence gathering, but could also include surveillance performed under strictly criminal investigations. The panel also held that "special needs" may also add justification for expanding FISA beyond its former limits. Attorney General Ashcroft welcomed the decision, calling it a "giant step forward."

The dramatic changes to U.S. surveillance law did not stop here. The USA PATRIOT Act introduced two novel search tools that would significantly increase the government's surveillance powers—the delayed notice search warrant and the national security letter. Delayed notice search warrants did away with the previous "knock and announce" standard, and required that government agents only demonstrate reasonable cause to believe that giving such notice would endanger the investigation, giving the government the ability to perform "sneak and peek" searches that would not tip off individuals to the fact that they were the subject of a search. National security letters (NSLs) enhanced the government's previous abilities to get around Fourth Amendment warrant requirements and forbade recipients of NSLs from advertising that fact. NSLs would become a particularly insidious part of post-9/11 surveillance, with ISPs, schools, libraries, and businesses receiving tens of thousands of these letters from government agencies every year, usually without any particularized suspicions about any individuals. For example, in the months following 9/11, libraries in the United States received more than 545 visits from federal agents, asking for information about their clients. Just a few NSLs issued to Las Vegas–area hotels yielded information on over 270,000 people, none of whom had been suspected of breaking any law.

In addition to applying pressure on Congress and the judiciary, the Bush administration also looked for novel interpretations of wartime surveillance powers within the executive branch. In the days and weeks following 9/11, it was generally understood within the White House that extraordinary measures were now required in order to effectively counter the threat of terrorism, both domestically and abroad. Riding this wave of reaction to the tragedies of September 2001, the Bush administration quickly—and secretly—established a program that authorized the NSA to begin conducting warrantless electronic surveillance that appeared to fall outside the restrictions laid out by FISA since 1978. This surveillance program cast a very wide net, and in doing so, captured purely domestic communications, which ran afoul of FISA restrictions on such foreign intelligence gathering. Attorney General Alberto Gonzales, who signed off on the legality of the program, authorized the interception of electronic communications whenever the government "has a reasonable basis to conclude that one party to the communication is a member of al Qaeda, affiliated with al Qaeda, or a member of an organization affiliated with al Qaeda, or working in support of al Qaeda," and another party to the communication is located "outside the United States."[3] The secret program was put into place in early 2002 during the U.S. government's early activities to locate and capture high-ranking al Qaeda members using their computer and cell phone communications. The scope of the surveilled network quickly ballooned to include thousands of people in the United States, and continued to grow until the program was revealed in December 2005 by the *New York Times*, which also stated that it had in fact obtained documentation of the program months earlier, but refrained from publishing because of pressure from the Bush administration. The heretofore secret program—now known as the Terrorist Surveillance Program (TSP)—became the basis for the first case to be evaluated by a court of appeals that directly challenged a government surveillance program in the post-9/11 era, forcing U.S. courts to reevaluate the standing doctrine that emerged from *Tatum* and its progeny.

On January 7, 2006, the American Civil Liberties Union (ACLU) along with eleven other organizations and individuals filed a complaint in the U.S. District Court for the Eastern District of Michigan, challenging the constitutionality of the TSP and alleging that the plaintiffs all had a "well-founded belief that their communications are being intercepted under the [TSP]," which "is disrupting the ability of the plaintiffs to talk with sources, locate witnesses, conduct scholarship, and engage in advocacy."[4] The government defendants, which included the NSA, argued that the state secrets privilege should bar the plaintiffs' claims, since without proof of the secret program they alleged injured them, they could not establish Article III standing. The *ACLU* court looked to the decision in *Halkin* and elsewhere for guidance on the application of the state secrets privilege, observing that the Bush administration's "War on Terror . . . has produced a vast number of cases, in which the state secrets privilege has been invoked." What set the present case apart from the others, however, was the fact that the government had asserted the privilege before any discovery requests had been made by the plaintiffs, thus appearing to argue that the privilege argument should not be subject to judicial review.

The *ACLU* court applied the test of state secrets assertions as first laid out in *Reynolds* and *Halkin*, and paused at the step that "determine[s] whether the information for which the privilege is claimed qualifies as a state secret"; after reviewing the documents presented by the defendants *in camera*, the court agreed with the defendants that the state secrets privilege applied to those documents "because a reasonable danger exists that disclosing the information in court proceedings would harm national security interests, or would impair national defense capabilities, disclose intelligence-gathering methods or capabilities, or disrupt diplomatic relations with foreign governments." But the plaintiffs pointed out that the information presented by the defendants for review was not relevant to the resolution of their claims, since they had been based solely on what the defendants had publicly admitted. The *ACLU* court thus drew a distinction between this case and *Halkin*, since the plaintiffs in the case before it were not actually seeking any additional discovery from the government defendants. The court recognized the simple fact that just because a statement is made public, it does not necessarily follow that that statement is true, but since the issue before the court was a threshold question of standing, and not a decision on the merits, the court upheld the plaintiffs' claims that did not depend on additional discovery. Defendants pointed out that this holding alone did not establish standing for the plaintiffs, and argued that their remaining claims were only of "subjective fear" of surveillance, which, under *Tatum*, falls short of the injury requirement to establish standing. The court held, however, that this case was distinguishable from *Tatum* because the *Tatum* plaintiffs "alleged only that they could *conceivably* become subject to the Army's domestic surveillance program," whereas the *ACLU* plaintiffs were "not merely alleging that they 'could conceivably' become subject to surveillance under the TSP, but that continuation of the TSP has damaged them." The district court therefore held that the plaintiffs had "sufficiently alleged that they suffered an actual, concrete injury traceable to Defendants and redressable by this court," and denied the defendants' motion to dismiss the plaintiffs' case for lack of standing.

The government defendants appealed the district court's decision, and the U.S. Court of Appeals for the Sixth Circuit took up the question of the ACLU's standing to bring its challenges of the TSP, since there is no "doctrine of hypothetical jurisdiction."[5] The appeals court acknowledged that the defendants' conduct giving rise to the alleged injuries was undisputed: "the NSA (1) eavesdrops, (2) without warrants, (3) on international telephone and email communications in which at least one of the parties is reasonably suspected of al Qaeda ties." But the plaintiffs did not present any evidence that their communications had ever been intercepted under the TSP—and in fact could not present this evidence due to the defendants' successful assertion of the state secrets privilege. Further, the plaintiffs did not allege "that they personally, either as individuals or associations, anticipate or fear any form of direct reprisal by the government (e.g., the NSA, the Justice Department, the Department of Homeland Security, etc.), such as criminal prosecution, deportation, administrative inquiry, civil litigation, or even public exposure." Rather, the plaintiffs' alleged injuries were subjective in nature, since they stemmed from the probabilistic argument that they would be surveilled (which, under the state secrets doctrine, none of them could prove), and their own reactions to that probability.

A careful observer of the chicken-and-egg reasoning that has grown from the *Tatum* decision regarding standing to challenge secret government surveillance programs might note at this point that the courts appear to be telling potential plaintiffs that, unless they willingly subject themselves to actual harms, such as arrest, loss of job, or some other measurable, specific negative result, it would be unlikely that any court would let them in the door to argue the merits of their case. The *ACLU* court addressed this question by explicitly stating that "[a] plaintiff's refusal to engage in potentially harmful activities . . . does not, by itself, preclude a finding that the plaintiff has standing." To understand how this rule applies, the court distinguished the two types of harm that enter this category. First, the "anticipated harm that *causes* one to refrain from the activities" can be held to satisfy the injury requirements of Article III standing doctrine only if that harm is imminent and concrete. The other type of harm is that which "*results* from refraining from the potentially harmful activities." Put simply, there is the harm that comes from the actions in question, and the harm that comes from avoiding those actions (in order to prevent the first kind of harm). The *ACLU* plaintiffs had argued that they were injured by this second kind of harm, since they "anticipate[d] that the NSA's interception of telephone and email communications might be detrimental to their overseas contacts, and this perceived harm causes the plaintiffs to refrain from that communication (i.e., potentially harmful activity)." But, since the state secrets privilege prevented them from proving the existence of the first kind of harm they were trying to avoid, and "proposing only injuries that result from this refusal to engage in communications (e.g., the inability to conduct their professions without added burden and expense)," they had offered only "an insufficient, speculative injury," which was not enough to support standing in their case. The *ACLU* court vacated the lower court's order and remanded the case with instructions to dismiss it for lack of standing. The *ACLU* plaintiffs appealed the decision to the Supreme Court, which denied certiorari.

The Sixth Circuit's divided decision in *ACLU* is a particularly apt Goldilocks-and-the-Three-Bears-style illustration of the judicial confusion that still remained over where to draw the line between chilling effect harms that meet the requirements of standing and those that do not, first suggested by *Tatum*. The author of the *ACLU* decision, Judge Alice M. Batchelder, adopted an expansive view of *Tatum*, which ruled out probabilistic claims of harm that arose from a fear of government surveillance. She observed that, while claims of First Amendment harms should be taken quite seriously by courts, the *ACLU* plaintiffs failed to show a sufficient amount of "probability or certainty" that their communications would be intercepted by the government under the TSP. But Batchelder's opinion also suggests that, even if the *ACLU* plaintiffs were able to prove somehow that their calls were, in fact, intercepted, their claims of First Amendment chill would be too "attenuated" an injury to permit Article III standing, since their fears arose merely from the government's retention—and possible future abuse—of their information, rather than from "direct government regulation, prescription, or compulsion." Further, even if the plaintiffs' claims of injury from First Amendment chilling were cognizable by the court, the specific program they challenged—the TSP—was not the cause of the injury, since secret (and legal) surveillance allowed under FISA would have also chilled their communications.

Judge Julia Gibbons concurred with Batchelder's judgment, but disagreed with her on the actual scope of *Tatum* with respect to chilled speech as cognizable injury. Diving into the series of important Supreme Court standing decisions from the 1980s and 1990s (see chapter 4), Gibbons observed that she did not share the expansive view of *Tatum* as standing for the preclusion of First Amendment chill from government surveillance as harm, but held firm on the sufficiency of imminent harm, stating that "it is the reality of the threat of repeated injury that is relevant to the standing inquiry, not the plaintiff's subjective apprehensions." Because the *ACLU* plaintiffs failed to show—due to the state secrets privilege—that they had been "personally subject" or "would be subject" to NSA surveillance under the TSP, this was not enough to meet the requirements of standing doctrine.

In his dissent, Judge Ronald Gilman articulated the narrow view of *Tatum*, stating that plaintiffs claiming injury from First Amendment chill from government surveillance do not have to show that they either had been or will be subject to the surveillance program in question; rather, the "reasonableness of their fear" of the effects of the surveillance was enough to support standing. To reach his conclusion, Gilman relied almost exclusively on the Supreme Court's decision in *Laidlaw* (see chapter 4), where the plaintiffs in that case had in fact been subject to the defendants' conduct, and argued that those plaintiffs were granted standing in that case because they reasonably feared injury arising from the defendants' conduct, and therefore, that "reasonable fear" was enough by itself to support Article III standing. Gilman pointed out that FISA required the government to minimize its collection, retention, and dissemination of information from surveillance, but the TSP did not appear to have these same restrictions. Thus, secret surveillance under FISA was legal, in part because of these restrictions, whereas TSP surveillance was enough of a question to instill a reasonable amount of fear in the *ACLU* plaintiffs.

These three opinions in *ACLU* illustrate the difficulties courts still had when applying *Tatum*. Specifically, courts appeared to be conflating the contexts of injury from Fourth Amendment–based and First Amendment–based harms. That is, injuries from surveillance could be seen as infringements of Fourth Amendment rights, where the government surveillance program could be argued to be an unreasonable search that did not follow constitutionally or statutorily required processes. These cases are generally argued in the context of challenges to the introduction of certain evidence, where both the target and the method of the search are known and uncontested. This is a breach of privacy claim, and aligns more closely with the first type of harm articulated by Judge Batchelder in *ACLU*. Under these circumstances, as the court points out, the plaintiff is required to produce evidence of the search or surveillance. But cases like *ACLU* are quite different. In this context, plaintiffs are not challenging unreasonable searches of individuals, but rather a secret program of surveillance that plaintiffs assert is operating outside the Constitution or statute, and these circumstances make it nearly impossible to meet the same kind of certainty requirements imposed on Fourth Amendment claimants. Should it be possible, where the precise targets of the surveillance cannot be known due to government secrecy, to modify the certainty requirements of standing doctrine, especially with respect to harm due to First Amendment chill? If the *Tatum* Court's decision regarding standing to bring such cases applied, where is the line that separates alleged harms from surveillance that meet the requirements for standing and those that do not, and when it comes to the chilling of First Amendment rights, does that line exist at all?

These questions formed the background context facing the Supreme Court in *Clapper v. Amnesty International*, the case first introduced in chapter 1 of this book.[6] Much like the plaintiffs in *ACLU*, the *Amnesty* plaintiffs were individuals and organizations who asserted that a secretly conducted government surveillance program had harmed them by unconstitutionally impairing their privacy and chilling their First Amendment rights. The program of surveillance the *Amnesty* plaintiffs were challenging was not the TSP this time, however, but rather a post-9/11 broadening of government surveillance powers through the FISA Amendments Act of 2008 (FAA).[7] The plaintiffs—attorneys, human rights advocates, and labor and media organizations—all required secure communications methods to protect their clients' dignity, attorney-client privilege, and sometimes even their physical safety, and because of the nature of these communications and the identities and geographic locations of some of these clients, the *Amnesty* plaintiffs held a reasonable belief that their communications were being intercepted, stored, and analyzed under the loosened surveillance rules of the FAA.

Prior to the FAA's passage, the rules set in place by FISA in 1978 generally forbade the government from engaging in electronic surveillance without first taking its request before the FISA court for its approval. This request must contain the identification of the surveillance target, the government's basis for believing that the target was either a foreign power or an agent of a foreign power, and a certification that a "significant purpose" of the surveillance was to obtain foreign intelligence information, among other specifics. Following the public exposure of the TSP in 2005, the Bush administration began work on a bill that would amend FISA to explicitly allow the surveillance activities the government had been secretly conducting since 2001. The White House submitted the bill, titled the Protect America Act of 2007 (PAA), to Congress on July 28, 2007; it rapidly passed both the House and Senate and was signed into law by President Bush on August 5, 2007. The PAA removed many of the important requirements of FISA, including the requirement that domestic communications not be targeted when collecting foreign intelligence information. Because of the PAA's controversial nature, the law contained language that would force its expiration six months after ratification. The PAA expired on February 17, 2008.

Anticipating the PAA's imminent expiration, the Bush administration and its allies in Congress had been working on replacement legislation that they hoped would continue allowing the expanded surveillance powers the PAA had granted the government. This bill—the FAA—contained language that was similar though not identical to that of the PAA, and included a provision that would permit the government to seek approval from the FISA court for surveillance designed to target thousands or even millions of communications. These mass surveillance orders still required the government to provide a certification to the court that its program was reasonably designed to ensure that the communications intercepts were "limited to targeting persons reasonably believed to be located outside the United States," and would "prevent the intentional acquisition of any communication as to which the sender and all intended recipients are known at the time of the acquisition to be located in the United States." The government would also be required to submit a list of "minimization procedures" to the court, which certifies the adoption of guidelines to ensure compliance with all legal limitations to government surveillance, including the Fourth Amendment, and that "a significant purpose of the acquisition is to obtain foreign intelligence information." Once such a mass surveillance order had been granted by the FISA court under the FAA, the government would be free to collect information via this surveillance program for up to one year before it would be required to seek reapproval from the court. The FAA was signed into law on July 10, 2008 by President Bush, who stated,

> The DNI and the Attorney General both report that, once enacted, this law will provide vital assistance to our intelligence officials in their work to thwart terrorist plots. This law will ensure that those companies whose assistance is necessary to protect the country will themselves be protected from lawsuits from past or future cooperation with the government. This law will protect the liberties of our citizens while maintaining the vital flow of intelligence.

The *Amnesty* plaintiffs could not have disagreed more. In their brief submitted to the Supreme Court, they asserted that just one of these mass surveillance orders, authorized under §1881(a) of FAA, could obtain, for example,

- all telephone and e-mail communications to and from countries of foreign policy interest—for example, Russia, Venezuela, or Israel—including communications made to and from U.S. citizens and residents;
- all telephone and e-mail communications to and from the leaders of the Pakistani lawyers' movement for democracy, with the specific purpose of learning whether those leaders are sharing information with American journalists and, if so, what information is being shared, and with which journalists; or
- all telephone and e-mail communications of European attorneys who work with American attorneys on behalf of prisoners held at Guantá-namo, including communications in which the two sets of attorneys share information about their clients and strategize about litigation.

These examples of possible mass surveillance orders, the plaintiffs argued, made it highly likely that their communications with their clients would be intercepted under the FAA's provisions. The plaintiffs had, therefore, been forced to take concrete steps to communicate through alternative and inconvenient channels due to their fear that their messages would be intercepted by the government under the FAA. When they brought their claims before the U.S. District Court for the Southern District of New York, that court, relying on the Sixth Circuit's decision in *ACLU*, held that the plaintiffs' fear of government surveillance alone was not a sufficient injury in fact to support standing. Upon appeal, however, the Second Circuit reversed the lower court's opinion, stating that

> the plaintiffs here have alleged that they reasonably anticipate direct injury from the enactment of the FAA because, unlike most Americans, *they engage in legitimate professional activities that make it reasonably likely that their privacy will be invaded and their conversations overheard—* unconstitutionally, or so they argue—as a result of the surveillance newly authorized by the FAA, and that they have already suffered tangible, indirect injury due to the reasonable steps they have undertaken to avoid

such overhearing, which would impair their ability to carry out those activities. (emphasis added)

The government defendants took their appeal to the Supreme Court, which granted certiorari on May 21, 2012.

On February 26, 2013, the Supreme Court released its decision in *Amnesty*, with Justice Samuel Alito writing for the majority. The Court firmly rejected the plaintiffs' argument that their allegations amounted to injury sufficient to confer Article III standing, which once again brought up the chicken-and-egg problem for future challenges to surveillance programs. Because the contested government surveillance programs had been conducted in secret, the plaintiffs were unable to provide concrete evidence that the government surveillance they feared was "certainly impending," and were thus unable to meet the standard for Article III standing articulated in *Tatum* and elsewhere. In his decision, Alito showed little patience for the Second Circuit's reasoning in this case:

> Respondents assert that they can establish injury in fact that is fairly traceable to §1881a because there is an objectively reasonable likelihood that their communications with their foreign contacts will be intercepted under §1881a at some point in the future. This argument fails. As an initial matter, the Second Circuit's "objectively reasonable likelihood" standard is inconsistent with our requirement that *threatened injury must be certainly impending to constitute injury in fact*. Furthermore, respondents' argument rests on their highly speculative fear that: (1) the Government will decide to target the communications of non-U.S. persons with whom they communicate; (2) in doing so, the Government will choose to invoke its authority under §1881a rather than utilizing another method of surveillance; (3) the Article III judges who serve on the Foreign Intelligence Surveillance Court will conclude that the Government's proposed surveillance procedures satisfy §1881a's many safeguards and are consistent with the Fourth Amendment; (4) the Government will succeed in intercepting the communications of respondents' contacts; and (5) respondents will be parties to the particular communications that the Government intercepts. *As discussed below, respondents' theory of standing, which relies on a highly attenuated chain of possibilities, does not satisfy the requirement that threatened injury must be certainly impending.* (emphasis added)

This reasoning, of course, left all such challenges to secret surveillance programs in the "highly speculative" category, since they would all face the same insurmountable evidentiary obstacle of proof of injury.

In his dissent, Justice Stephen Breyer pointed directly at this closed logical loop, and argued that some degree of probability based on inference and common sense should be able to break that loop and find standing in some such surveillance cases. But Alito's newly articulated standard, which required a plaintiff's injury to be "certainly impending" to support standing, appeared to make this loop permanently closed. Breyer observed that

> certainty is not, and never has been, the touchstone of standing. The future is inherently uncertain. Yet federal courts frequently entertain actions for injunctions and for declaratory relief aimed at preventing future activities that are reasonably likely or highly likely, but not absolutely certain, to take place. And that degree of certainty is all that is needed to support standing here.

In fact, Breyer pointed out, the Supreme Court had granted Article III standing to claims that were at least as probabilistic as the ones currently before it: "[T]he Court has often *found* standing where the occurrence of the relevant injury was far less certain than here," and had even "found *probabilistic* injuries sufficient to support standing" (emphasis in original). The bottom line for Breyer was the insurmountability of the obstacle Alito appeared to be setting in front of future challenges to secret government surveillance programs:

> In sum, as the Court concedes, the word "certainly" in the phrase "certainly impending" does not refer to absolute certainty. As our case law demonstrates, what the Constitution requires is something more akin to "reasonable probability" or "high probability." The use of some such standard is all that is necessary here to ensure the actual concrete injury that the Constitution demands. The considerations . . . make clear that the standard is readily met in this case.

Rather than offer greater clarity on the issue of standing, the Supreme Court's decision in *Amnesty* appeared thus to erect an unscalable wall preventing future plaintiffs from challenging secret surveillance programs (or even arguing the merits of their claims). But shortly after the Court's decision was published, a former NSA employee named Edward Snowden appeared on the scene as something of a *deus ex machina*. In June 2013 the *Washington Post* reported that Snowden had made off with a collection of secret government documents that appeared to reveal a number of secret—and possibly illegal—surveillance programs, some of which hewed quite closely to the descriptions alleged by the *ACLU* and *Amnesty* plaintiffs. Among the documents revealed by Snowden was a description of a program called PRISM, which (internally) advertised itself as permissible under the FAA. Upon learning of this program, Senator Mark Udall observed that "there is nothing to prohibit the intelligence community from searching through a pile of communications, which may have been incidentally or accidentally been collected without a warrant, to deliberately search for the phone calls or e-mails of specific Americans." Indeed, the Snowden documents seemed to confirm the *Amnesty* plaintiffs' fears, but would a post-Snowden judiciary treat the *Tatum* standing doctrine any differently?

9

The Future of Citizen Challenges to Government Surveillance

When I first began the research for this book, the question of Article III standing to challenge secret government surveillance programs appeared to be entering unexplored territory. The Snowden revelations, which began in June 2013, opened up a world of detail about hundreds of secret surveillance programs, and discussions began to percolate as to the effects these revelations might have on the standing issue. As scholars and experts from a wide array of disciplines began to sift through the released documents, a picture began to emerge of a global surveillance state that was much larger and more complex than previously imagined. Of particular interest to many attorneys and advocacy groups was the extent to which the NSA had expanded its domestic surveillance programs. Included among the many documents in this category was an order from the FISA court, under the PRISM program, requiring Verizon Business Network Services to turn over telephone call data, including details on who placed calls to whom, when the calls were made, and how long each call lasted, on "an ongoing daily basis." Similar orders were also discovered for Google, Yahoo, Facebook, Twitter, Dropbox, and Apple. While the information to be collected did not include the actual content of the communications at issue, these "metadata" could reveal quite a large number of details about someone, even without the benefit of eavesdropping on the conversation itself.

This outlook has not historically been shared by U.S. courts, however. The case that first took a hard look at the issue of metadata was the Supreme Court's 1979 decision in *Smith v. Maryland*, which held that it was not a "search" under the Fourth Amendment for the government to ask a telephone company to record and report the incoming and outgoing calls from a particular telephone number, since there was no reasonable expectation of privacy (applying *Katz*, discussed in chapter 6) held in information that has been voluntarily given to a third party—a telephone company, in this example.[1] As the *Smith* Court reasoned,

> Telephone users, in sum, typically know that they must convey numerical information to the phone company; that the phone company has facilities for recording this information; and that the phone company does in fact record this information for a variety of legitimate business purposes. Although subjective expectations cannot be scientifically gauged, it is too much to believe that telephone subscribers, under these circumstances, harbor any general expectation that the numbers they dial will remain secret.

The Court's decision in *Smith* became the basis for the "third party doctrine," still applied today, which holds that those who voluntarily give up information to a third party have no reasonable expectation of privacy in that shared information, which therefore can be provided to the government without the need for a warrant. Examples of such "voluntarily shared information" have included bank records, email header information, and cell phone location data.

As technologies have advanced, however, some courts are beginning to question the scope of the third party doctrine as it applies to twenty-first-century communications. For example, in the 2012 case of *United States v. Jones*, the Supreme Court held that installing a Global Positioning System (GPS) tracking device on a car in order to monitor its movements is a "search" under the Fourth Amendment, and therefore requires a warrant.[2] But the opinion that drew the most attention in this case was Justice Sonia Sotomayor's concurrence, where she wrote that "it may be necessary to reconsider the premise" of the third party doctrine:

> This approach is ill suited to the digital age, in which people reveal a great deal of information about themselves to third parties in the course of carrying out mundane tasks. People disclose the phone numbers that they dial or text to their cellular providers; the URLs that they visit and the e-mail addresses with which they correspond to their Internet service providers; and the books, groceries, and medications they purchase to online retailers. Perhaps, as Justice Alito notes, some people may find the "tradeoff" of privacy for convenience "worthwhile," or come to accept

this "diminution of privacy" as "inevitable," and perhaps not. I for one doubt that people would accept without complaint the warrantless disclosure to the Government of a list of every Web site they had visited in the last week, or month, or year. But whatever the societal expectations, they can attain constitutionally protected status only if our Fourth Amendment jurisprudence ceases to treat secrecy as a prerequisite for privacy.

In fact, Sotomayor argued, the monitoring of location metadata can be especially invasive:

> In cases involving even short-term monitoring, some unique attributes of GPS surveillance relevant to the Katz analysis will require particular attention. GPS monitoring generates a precise, comprehensive record of a person's public movements that reflects a wealth of detail about her familial, political, professional, religious, and sexual associations. See, e.g., People v. Weaver, 909 N. E. 2d 1195, 1199 (N.Y. 2009) *("Disclosed in [GPS] data . . . will be trips the indisputably private nature of which takes little imagination to conjure: trips to the psychiatrist, the plastic surgeon, the abortion clinic, the AIDS treatment center, the strip club, the criminal defense attorney, the by-the-hour motel, the union meeting, the mosque, synagogue or church, the gay bar and on and on")*. The Government can store such records and efficiently mine them for information years into the future. And because GPS monitoring is cheap in comparison to conventional surveillance techniques and, by design, proceeds surreptitiously, it evades the ordinary checks that constrain abusive law enforcement practices: "limited police resources and community hostility." (emphasis added)

When Elliot Schuchardt, an attorney in Pittsburgh, first read of the Snowden revelations, and in particular, PRISM and its wide scope, it occurred to him that his communications could very likely be swept up in this bulk surveillance program. In fact, it was probable that many Americans could be subject to this mass collection of data, without their knowledge and outside the protections of the Fourth Amendment. On June 2, 2015, Schuchardt filed a complaint in the U.S. District Court for the Western District of Pennsylvania on behalf of himself and a nationwide class of similarly situations persons "defined as: American citizens who are subscribers, users, and/or consumers of the internet services of

Google, Yahoo, and Facebook, the cloud storage services of Dropbox, and the telecommunication services of Verizon." Schuchardt sought injunctive relief, an order to prevent further collection under the program, a determination of the maximum duration for storage under the FISA minimization procedures, actual or statutory damages, and attorney fees.

Unsurprisingly, the preliminary question before the district court in *Schuchardt v. Obama* was that of Article III standing, with the court going directly to *ACLU* and *Amnesty* for guidance.[3] With respect to the standing doctrine's injury-in-fact requirement, the *Schuchardt* court provided a somewhat crude summary of the distinction that appeared to be emerging in contemporary surveillance cases:

> In situations where plaintiffs are able to allege with some degree of particularity that their own communications were specifically targeted—for example, by citing a leaked FISC order or relying on a detailed insider account—courts have concluded that the particularity requirement has been satisfied. On the other hand, courts have refused to find standing based on naked averments that an individual's communications must have been seized because the government operates a data collection program and the individual utilized the service of a large telecommunications company or companies.

Finding that the plaintiff "falls squarely within the second category" because of his "reliance on publicly available information, only," and that he had "identified no facts from which the Court reasonably might infer that his own communications have been targeted, seized or stored," the *Schuchardt* court denied standing. Schuchardt appealed the district court decision to the U.S. Court of Appeals for the Third Circuit, arguing that the lower court misapplied Article III standing precedent.

The appeals court, observing that "Schuchardt's appeal is the latest in a line of cases raising the question of a plaintiff's standing to challenge surveillance authorized by [the FAA]," singled out the "dispositive question" that faced the courts in *ACLU* and *Amnesty*, which was "whether the plaintiffs had established an 'imminent' injury 'fairly traceable' to the government's conduct." The *Schuchardt* court also noted that, since the decisions in *ACLU* and *Amnesty*, "former NSA contractor Edward Snowden leaked a trove of classified documents to journalists writing for the *Washington Post* and *Guardian*" that "referenced the existence of an NSA program engaged in the bulk collection of domestic telephone metadata, i.e., details about telephone calls, including for example, the length of a call, the phone number from which the call was made, and the phone number called, but not the voice content of the call itself." One of these documents, the court observed, suggested a slogan for the NSA's post-9/11 "New Collection Posture": "Sniff it All, Know it All, Collect it All, Process it All, Exploit it All, and Partner it All."

Starting with this post-Snowden context and "first principles," the *Schuchardt* court stated that the plaintiff's "Article III standing turns on two inquiries. First, were his allegations sufficiently 'particularized' to demonstrate that he suffered a discrete injury? Second, were those facts pleaded with enough detail to render them plausible, 'well-pleaded' allegations entitled to a presumption of truth?" Regarding the first question, the *Schuchardt* court looked to *Hassan v. City of New York*, a case it had recently decided, where the plaintiffs there challenged a New York City Police Department surveillance program implemented "to monitor the lives of Muslims, their businesses, houses of worship, organizations, and schools."[4] Like the *Hassan* plaintiffs, Schuchardt had "alleged a program of government surveillance that, though universal in scope, is unmistakably personal in the purported harm." The collected information "allegedly encompasses Schuchardt's personal communications, and includes not only the kind of intensely private details that one could reasonably expect to find in the email accounts of most Americans—'bank account numbers; credit card numbers; passwords for financial data; [and] health records'— but also data influenced by Schuchardt's personal circumstances, namely 'trade secrets' and 'communications with clients of Schuchardt's law firm, which are privileged and confidential under applicable law.'" As the court held in *Hassan*, it also held that Schuchardt's allegations were sufficient to demonstrate particularized injury under Article III.

The second inquiry—whether Schuchardt's allegations should be credited as true for the purposes of the question of standing—the court turned to the precedents set by *Ashcroft v. Iqbal* and *Bell Atl. Corp. v. Twombly*, which clarified pleading requirements such that a "plausibility determination is a context-specific task that requires the reviewing court to draw on its judicial experience and common sense."[5] In response to Schuchardt's assertion that the district court had applied an artificially (and incorrect) heightened pleading standard to his case, the appeals court stated that this was "unclear," but also observed that the *Hassan* plaintiffs, under similar circumstances, had "plausibly pleaded both their standing to sue and claims for relief." The plausibility of Schuchardt's alleged injuries, therefore, "depend[ed] on the plausibility of his assertion that PRISM functions as an indiscriminate dragnet which captures all or substantially all of the e-mail sent by American citizens." The *Schuchardt* court found that he had "outlined a coherent and plausible case supporting his PRISM-as-dragnet allegations," which were "replete with details confirming PRISM's operational scope and capabilities," and "support [his] allegation that the scope of PRISM's data collection encompasses his personal email." This all appeared quite positive for the plaintiff, but the final opinion of the *Schuchardt* court was an explicitly narrow one:

> [W]e hold only that Schuchardt's second amended complaint pleaded his standing to sue for a violation of his Fourth Amendment right to be free from unreasonable searches and seizures. *This does not mean that he has standing to sue*, as the Government remains free upon remand to make a factual jurisdictional challenge to Schuchardt's pleading. In anticipation of such a challenge, we provide the following guidance to the District Court on remand. (emphasis added)

In other words, Schuchardt's case lived on to fight another day, but given the precedents that have been set since *Tatum*, the road forward appears entirely uphill.

New challenges to government surveillance programs continue to be brought before federal courts as well. For example, in March 2015 the Wikimedia Foundation, Human Rights Watch, the National Association of Criminal Defense Lawyers, and other human rights and media groups filed a complaint in the U.S. District Court for the District of Maryland, alleging that they had been harmed by the NSA's "upstream" surveillance program.[6] The NSA's upstream surveillance collects all international communications, emails, browsing activity, and web searches, by tapping into the Internet's "backbone" to monitor traffic as it exits and enters the country. The government responded by asserting that upstream surveillance was completely legal under the FISA Amendments Act of

2008. Apart from these technical details, the *Wikimedia* case was quite similar to the facts of the *Amnesty* case. The district court, applying *Amnesty*, dismissed the *Wikimedia* plaintiffs' complaint for lack of standing, noting in dicta that while "no government surveillance program should be immunized from judicial scrutiny," the plaintiffs' concerns were misplaced, since the FISA Court reviews all such programs (albeit secretly). The *Wikimedia* plaintiffs appealed this decision to the Court of Appeals for the Fourth Circuit, and oral argument was scheduled for December 2016.

On May 23, 2017, the Fourth Circuit unanimously reversed a part of the district court's dismissal of the *Wikimedia* complaint, holding that Wikimedia has standing to proceed in the case, as it had

> plausibly alleged that its communications travel all of the roads that a communication can take, and that the NSA seizes all of the communications along at least one of those roads. Thus, at least at this stage of the litigation, Wikimedia has standing to sue for a violation of the Fourth Amendment. And, because Wikimedia has self-censored its speech and sometimes forgone electronic communications in response to [NSA] surveillance, it also has standing to sue for a violation of the First Amendment.[7]

The "speculative" nature of the injuries that caused the Supreme Court in *Clapper v. Amnesty Int'l* to hold that the plaintiffs in that case had failed to establish Article III standing, upon which the district court in *Wikimedia* relied, did not apply to Wikimedia in the present case. As Judge Ellis wrote in the court's opinion, "there's nothing speculative about it—the interception of Wikimedia's communications is an actual injury that has already occurred." Two of the three judges on the panel found that the other plaintiffs lacked standing, although Judge Davis, in his dissent, argued that all nine plaintiffs should be granted standing. The Fourth Circuit thus reversed the lower court's dismissal of the complaint as to Wikimedia—and only Wikimedia—and remanded the case back to the district court to continue proceedings consistent with the appeals court's opinion.

As this book goes to print, the question therefore remains: Have the family of cases from *Tatum* to *Lujan, ACLU*, and *Amnesty* created an insurmountable obstacle for challenges to secret surveillance programs in U.S. courts, or have the recent developments in the *Wikimedia* case given potential plaintiffs a road map toward convincing courts of actual, non-speculative injuries? And what injuries must plaintiffs plead in order to get past the standing question to the actual merits of their case? Is a reasonable likelihood enough, or must the harm be "certainly impending"? The chicken-and-egg dilemma appears to be alive and well. Plaintiffs seeking to challenge secret government surveillance programs may not have enough evidence to show injury in fact, and are forbidden from obtaining this evidence based on the secrecy of the program itself. Unless and until there is a seismic shift in the Supreme Court's understanding of Article III standing doctrine, including, perhaps, an overturning of *Tatum*, it may not be possible for plaintiffs to have their surveillance challenges heard in U.S. courts.

NOTES

CHAPTER 1. YOU ARE BEING WATCHED

1 Author interview with Joanne Mariner, Dec. 18, 2014, on file with author.

2 U.S. SENATE SELECT COMMITTEE ON INTELLIGENCE, COMMITTEE STUDY OF THE CENTRAL INTELLIGENCE AGENCY'S DETENTION AND INTERROGATION PROGRAM, S. REP. NO. 113–288 (2014), www.intelligence. senate.gov; also available at https://web.archive.org.

3 *See* Public Unredacted Klein Declaration, Hepting v. AT&T, 439 F. Supp. 2d 974 (N.D. Cal. 2006), www.eff.org.

4 It should be noted here that light is itself a form of electromagnetic radiation, but we shall not quibble over the details of the electromagnetic spectrum here, as it is beyond the scope of this work.

5 Hepting v. AT&T, 439 F. Supp. 2d 974 (N.D. Cal. 2006).

6 Jewel v. NSA, 2010 U.S. Dist. LEXIS 5110 (N.D. Cal. 2010).

7 In later chapters, we will explore the use of the term "collecting"—especially as used by the intelligence community—more fully.

8 The original case was brought as Amnesty International et al. v. McConnell, but the named defendants changed when James Clapper took over as director of national intelligence (DNI).

CHAPTER 2. A HISTORY OF GOVERNMENT SURVEILLANCE

1 CAROL REARDON, SOLDIERS AND SCHOLARS (1990) 102–4.

2 REARDON at 37.

3 *See Federal Data Banks, Computers and the Bill of Rights: Hearings Before the Subcommittee on Constitutional Rights of the Committee on the Judiciary*, 92d Cong., 1st Sess. Part I at 147 (1971) (statement of Christopher H. Pyle, Attorney, and Former Captain in Army Intelligence).

4 *See* Christopher H. Pyle, *CONUS Revisited: The Army Covers Up*, WASHINGTON MONTHLY, Jul. 1970, at 49.

5 *See* CONG. REC., 91st Cong., 2nd sess., 2227.

6 *See* Pyle, *CONUS Revisited, supra.*

7 *See id.*

8 *See id.*

9 *See id.*

CHAPTER 3. GETTING THROUGH THE COURTHOUSE DOOR

1 *See* Arlo Tatum, *A Second Time Around, in* FREE RADICALS: WAR RESISTERS IN PRISON (C. J. Hinke, 2017), www.wri-irg.org.

2 *See Curbs on Freedom by States Feared*, N.Y. TIMES, Jan. 2, 1941, at 8.

3 Francis Biddle, *Civil Rights in Times of Stress*, 2 BILL RTS. REV. 13 (1941).

4 Francis Biddle, *The Power of Democracy: It Can Meet All Conditions*, VITAL SPEECHES, Oct. 15, 1941.

5 Cabell Phillips, *No Witch Hunts*, N.Y. TIMES MAGAZINE, Sep. 21, 1941.

6 RICHARD W. STEELE, FREE SPEECH IN THE GOOD WAR (1999) 121.

7 Tatum v. Laird, Civil No. 459-70 (D.D.C. 1970).

8 It is worth noting that despite the Army's claims of constitutionality and its motion to dismiss the plaintiffs' complaint under FRCP Rule 12(b)(6), an affidavit presented by Undersecretary of the Army Thaddeus Beal did state that "[a]s a result of a review of the intelligence activities of the U.S. Army it has been determined that certain records maintained by the Army were not useful and were not necessary in view of the Army's mission."

9 DAVID RUDENSTINE, THE DAY THE PRESSES STOPPED (1996) 391. Judge Hart presided over a number of high-profile, politically charged cases during his tenure on the bench. In 1971 Hart granted an injunction preventing the protest group Vietnam Veterans Against the War from building a mock encampment on the Mall in front of the U.S. Capitol Building. The injunction was overturned by the U.S. Court of Appeals for the D.C. Circuit, only to be reestablished by Chief Justice Warren Burger in his capacity as circuit justice for the District of Columbia. Despite all of this, the Department of Justice failed to enforce the injunction, enraging Judge Hart, who told government lawyers that he felt "used" by the executive branch of government.

10 Tatum v. Laird, 444 F.2d 947 (D.C. Cir. 1971).

11 5 U.S. 1 (1 Cranch) 137 (1803).

12 United States v. Klein (1872) is the single exception to this rule.

13 21 CONG. REC. 10,222 (1890).

14 William H. Taft, *The Attacks on the Courts and Legal Procedure*, 5 KY. L.J. 18 (Nov. 1916).

15 277 U.S. 438 (1928).

16 Sup. Ct. R. 14(1)(a).

17 Yee v. City of Escondido, 503 U.S. 519 (1992).

18 *See* Commonwealth Coatings v. Continental Casualty Co., 393 U.S. 145 (1968) (the Court stating that the "canon of judicial ethics rest on the premise that any tribunal permitted by law to try cases and controversies not only must be unbiased but also must avoid even the appearance of bias").

19 *See* In re Murchison, 349 U.S. 133 (1955).

CHAPTER 4. THE DOCTRINE OF ARTICLE III STANDING

1 Valley Forge Christian College v. Americans United for Separation of Church and State, Inc., 454 U.S. 464, 471 (1982). The relevant section of the Constitution ("Jurisdiction of Courts") reads as follows:

Section 2. The judicial Power shall extend to all Cases, in Law and Equity, arising under this Constitution, the Laws of the United States, and Treaties made, or which shall be made, under their Authority;—to all Cases affecting Ambassadors, other public Ministers and Consuls;—to all Cases of admiralty and maritime Jurisdiction;—to Controversies to which the United States shall be a Party;—to Controversies between two or more States;—between a State and Citizens of another State;—between Citizens of different States;— between Citizens of the same State claiming Lands under Grants of different States, and between a State, or the Citizens thereof, and foreign States, Citizens or Subjects.

U.S.C.A. Const. Art. III § 2, cl. 1.

2 D. E. Ho & E. L. Ross, *Did Liberal Justices Invent the Standing Doctrine? An Empirical Study of the Evolution of Standing, 1921–2006*, 62 STANFORD L. REV. 591 (2010).

3 *See, e.g.*, Cass R. Sunstein, *Standing and the Privatization of Public Law*, 88 COLUM. L. REV. 1432 (1988). We will explore this intriguing prospect later in this chapter.

4 *See, e.g.*, Gene R. Nichol Jr., *Abusing Standing: A Comment on* Allen v. Wright, 133 U. PA. L. REV. 635 (1985).

5 JOSEPH VINING, LEGAL IDENTITY: THE COMING OF AGE OF PUBLIC LAW (1978).

6 Allen v. Wright, 468 U.S. 737 (1984).

7 Bob Jones Univ. v. United States, 461 U.S. 574 (1983).

8 Flast v. Cohen, 392 U.S. 83 (1968).

9 *Id.*

10 Muskrat v. United States, 219 U.S. 346 (1911).

11 United States v. Johnson, 319 U.S. 302 (1943).

12 Baker v. Carr, 369 U.S. 186 (1962).

13 Valley Forge Christian College v. Americans United for Separation of Church and State, Inc., 454 U.S. 464 (1982).

14 Warth v. Seldin, 422 U.S. 490 (1975).

15 Allen v. Wright, 468 U.S. at 641.

16 42 U.S.C.A. § 7604.

17 33 U.S.C.A. § 1365

18 *See, e.g.*, NRDC v. Train, 396 F. Supp. 1393 (1975).

19 Gwaltney of Smithfield, Ltd. v. Chesapeake Bay Foundation, Inc., 484 U.S. 49 (1987).

20 Antonin Scalia, *The Doctrine of Standing as an Essential Element of the Separation of Powers*, 17 SUFFOLK U. L. REV. 881 (1983).

21 Lujan v. National Wildlife Federation, 497 U.S. 871 (1990).

22 5 U.S.C.A. § 702.

23 Lujan v. Defenders of Wildlife, 504 U.S. 555 (1992).

24 16 U.S.C.A. § 1540(g).

25 New York Times Co. v. Sullivan, 376 U.S. 254 (1964).

26 Dombrowski v. Pfister, 380 U.S. 479 (1965).

CHAPTER 5. BEFORE THE SUPREME COURT

1 *See generally* JOHN W. DEAN, THE REHNQUIST CHOICE: THE UNTOLD STORY OF THE NIXON APPOINTMENT THAT REDEFINED THE SUPREME COURT (2001).

2 *Id.* at 86.

3 *See Federal Data Banks, supra*, at 600–604.

4 William H. Rehnquist, Privacy, Surveillance, and the Law, Remarks before the National Conference of Law Reviews, Williamsburg, Va. (Mar. 19, 1971) (reprinted in *id.* at 1590–96).

5 *Federal Data Banks, supra*, at 603.

6 *Id.* at 864–65. The use of the term "lie" may appear unusual to those not previously exposed to this legal term of art. Here, "an action will lie" simply means that an action can be sustained or that there are grounds up on which the action may be founded.

7 Lawrence M. Baskir, *Reflections on the Senate Investigation of Army Surveillance*, 49 IND. L.J. 618, 643–45 (1973).

8 Laird v. Tatum, Oral Argument, Mar. 27, 1972.

9 Bivens v. Six Unknown Named Agents, 403 U.S. 388 (1971).

10 Gray v. Sanders, 372 U.S. 368 (1963).

11 10 U.S.C.S. § 331. "Whenever there is an insurrection in any State against its government, the President may, upon the request of its legislature or of its governor if the legislature cannot be convened, call into Federal service such of the militia of the other States, in the number requested by that State, and use such of the armed forces, as he considers necessary to suppress the insurrection."

12 Department of the Army, *Civil Disturbance Plan*, Sep. 10, 1968.

13 *FBI Director Hits Selfish Few*, CHICAGO TRIBUNE, Nov. 25, 1964.

14 FBI Memorandum re Counterintelligence Program: Black Nationalist—Hate Groups; Internal Security, Aug. 25, 1967, https://vault.fbi.gov.

15 SELECT COMM. TO STUDY GOVERNMENTAL OPERATIONS WITH RESPECT TO INTELLIGENCE ACTIVITIES, 94TH CONG., FINAL REPORT ON INTELLIGENCE ACTIVITIES AND THE RIGHTS OF AMERICANS, Book II, 17 (1976), www.intelligence.senate.gov.

16 *See* Baskir, *Reflections, supra*.

17 In re Murchison, 349 U.S. 133 (1955).

18 *Id.*

19 28 U.S.C.S. § 455 (1968).

20 United States v. Amerine, 411 F.2d 1130 (6th Cir. 1969).

21 Laird v. Tatum, 409 U.S. 824 (1972).

CHAPTER 6. GOVERNMENT SURVEILLANCE AND THE LAW

1 McCulloch v. Maryland, 17 U.S. 316 (1819).

2 Cohens v. Virginia, 19 U.S. 264 (1821).

3 Cherokee Nation v. Georgia, 30 U.S. 1 (1831).

4 Prigg v. Pennsylvania, 41 U.S. 539 (1842).

5 *See, e.g.*, Ableman v. Booth, 62 U.S. 506 (1859) (holding that a state supreme court lacked jurisdiction to discharge a prisoner convicted under federal law of aiding and abetting the escape of a fugitive slave).

6 *See, e.g.*, Slaughter-House Cases, 83 U.S. 36 (1872) (interpreting the then recently passed Fourteenth Amendment as protecting the "privileges or immunities" conferred on U.S. citizens, and not protecting rights associated with citizenship of a state).

7 *See, e.g.*, Konigsberg v. State Bar of Cal., 353 U.S. 252 (1957) (holding that the mere fact that someone was a past member of the Communist Party was not an adequate basis for concluding that an applicant to the state bar was of bad moral character).

8 United States v. Olmstead, 7 F.2d 760 (W.D. Wash. 1925).

9 Olmstead v. United States, 19 F.2d 842 (9th Cir. 1927).

10 276 U.S. 609 (1928).

11 Prigg v. Pennsylvania, 41 U.S. 539 (1842).

12 Ex parte Jackson, 96 U.S. 727 (1877).

13 Boyd v. United States, 116 U.S. 616 (1886).

14 Scott v. Sandford, 60 U.S. 393 (1856).

15 Plessy v. Ferguson, 163 U.S. 537 (1896).

16 Brown v. Board of Education of Topeka, 347 U.S. 483 (1954).

17 4 HARV. L. REV. 193 (1890).

18 Pierce v. United States, 252 U.S. 239 (1920).

19 Gilbert v. Minnesota, 254 U.S. 325 (1920).

20 JOAN JENSEN, ARMY SURVEILLANCE IN AMERICA (1991) 128.

21 Federal Communications Act of 1934, 48 Stat. 1103 (1934) (amended by 47 U.S.C. 605 (1968)).

22 McDonald v. United States, 335 U.S. 451 (1948).

23 Johnson v. United States, 333 U.S. 10 (1948).

24 Katz v. United States, 389 U.S. 347 (1967).

25 The court record does not explain why the FBI agents did not simply place microphones on all three of the telephone booths. It may have been the case that the FBI had only two microphones in its inventory.

26 United States v. United States Dist. Court (*Keith* case), 407 U.S. 297 (1972).

27 United States v. United States Dist. Court, 444 F.2d 651 (1971).

28 Youngstown Sheet & Tube Co. v. Sawyer, 343 U.S. 579 (1952).

CHAPTER 7. THE LEGACY OF *LAIRD V. TATUM*

 1 Finley v. Hampton, 473 F.2d 180 (D.C. Cir. 1972); Donohoe v. Duling, 465 F.2d 196 (4th Cir. 1972); American Civil Liberties Union v. Laird, 463 F.2d 499 (7th Cir. 1972). It is worth noting that the court in *ACLU v. Laird* had expressly deferred its final decision until after the Supreme Court rendered its opinion in *Tatum*.

 2 5 U.S.C. § 552a.

 3 Handschu v. Special Services Div., 349 F. Supp. 766 (S.D.N.Y. 1972).

 4 480 F.2d 326 (2d. Cir. 1973).

 5 Philadelphia Resistance v. Mitchell, 58 F.R.D 139 (E.D. Pa. 1972). For rules governing pretrial discovery, see Fed. R. Civ. P. 37 (Failure to Make Disclosures or to Cooperate in Discovery, Sanctions).

 6 407 F. Supp. 115 (N.D. Ill. 1975).

 7 Socialist Workers Party v. Attorney Gen., 419 U.S. 1314 (1972).

 8 The *Socialist Workers Party* Court ultimately denied the plaintiffs' request to stay the Second Circuit's decision and reinstate the district court's original injunction, however, based on their failure to bring a compelling case on the merits. Since "the nature of the proposed monitoring [was] limited, the conduct [was] entirely legal, and if relief were granted, the potential injury to the FBI's continuing investigative efforts would be apparent," and since "the Court of Appeals has already granted interim relief" regarding the "threat of disclosure of names to the Civil Service Commission," the Court was "reluctant to upset the judgment of the Court of Appeals."

 9 The Pike Committee Report was never officially released but was published in part in the *Village Voice* on February 16, 1976, and later as a book in the United Kingdom in 1977. CIA, THE PIKE REPORT (1977).

10 Jabara v. Kelley, 476 F. Supp. 561 (E.D. Mich. 1979).

11 Jabara v. Webster, 691 F.2d 272 (6th Cir. 1982). Note that the first named defendant changed to reflect the fact that William Webster had been named the director of the FBI in the interim between the trial and the appeal.

12 Halkin v. Helms, 598 F.2d 1 (D.C. Cir. 1978) (citations omitted).

13 Halkin v. Helms, 690 F.2d 977, 990 (D.C. Cir. 1982).

14 United States v. Reynolds, 345 U.S. 1 (1953).

15 It seems, however that the facts in *Reynolds*, once declassified, did not appear to support the government's claim of state secrets privilege. Years after the decision, it was revealed that the official Air Force report, withheld from evidence by the *Reynolds* Court under the state secrets privilege, did not contain information regarding secret electronic equipment, which was the very information alleged by the government to be subject to the privilege. *See* LOUIS FISHER, IN THE NAME OF NATIONAL SECURITY: UNCHECKED PRESIDENTIAL POWER AND THE REYNOLDS CASE (2006).

16 Halkin v. Helms, 690 F.2d 977 (D.C. Cir. 1982).

17 Halkin v. Helms, 598 F.2d 1 (D.C. Cir. 1978).

18 United Presbyterian Church v. Reagan, 738 F.2d 1375 (D.C. Cir. 1984).

CHAPTER 8. TECHNOLOGY, NATIONAL SECURITY, AND SURVEILLANCE

1 The writ of habeas corpus is a legal privilege whereby one can report or contest an unlawful detention or imprisonment by the government, and is the only such privilege that is explicitly articulated in the Constitution, which also lays out limited circumstances for its suspension when in "Cases of Rebellion or Invasion the public Safety may require it." With no small amount of controversy, the federal government suspended habeas corpus during the Civil War and Reconstruction, and curtailed the privilege during World War II.

2 The full name of this was the improbable Uniting and Strengthening America by Providing Appropriate Tools Required to Intercept and Obstruct Terrorism Act of 2001, mercifully shortened to the USA PATRIOT Act of 2001, Pub L. No. 107–56, 18 U.S.C. 214 (2000).

3 James Risen and Eric Lichtblau, *Bush Lets U.S. Spy on Callers without Courts*, N.Y. Times, Dec. 16, 2005.

4 Complaint, ACLU v. Nat'l Sec. Agency/Central Sec. Serv., 438 F. Supp. 2d 754 (E.D. Mich. 2006).

5 ACLU v. NSA, 493 F.3d 644 (6th Cir. 2007).

6 133 S. Ct. 1138 (2013).

7 Pub L. No. 110–261 (2008), codified at 50 U.S.C. 1881a et seq.

CHAPTER 9. THE FUTURE OF CITIZEN CHALLENGES TO GOVERNMENT SURVEILLANCE

1 442 U.S. 735 (1979).

2 132 S. Ct. 945 (2012).

3 2015 WL 5732117 (Sep. 30, 2015).

4 804 F.3d 277 (3d Cir. Oct. 13, 2015).

5 Ashcroft v. Iqbal, 556 U.S. 662 (2009); Bell Atl. Corp. v. Twombly, 550 U.S. 544 (2007).

6 Wikimedia Found. v. NSA/Central Sec. Serv., 143 F. Supp. 3d 344 (D. Md. 2015).

7 Wikimedia Found. v. NSA/Central Sec. Serv., Case No. 15–2560 (4th Cir. May 23, 2017), available at https://assets.documentcloud.org.

INDEX

ABOUT THE AUTHOR

Jeffrey L. Vagle is Lecturer in Law and Executive Director of the Center for Technology, Innovation and Competition at the University of Pennsylvania Law School. His research interests include surveillance law, cryptography and cybersecurity law, electronic privacy, Internet architecture, and networked economies and societies. A particular focus of his work is the study of the societal, political, historical, and economic effects of government surveillance, especially among marginalized or disenfranchised populations.